"This timely book makes the case for the important role that M&A plays in fostering profitable growth in these turbulent times. It is chock-full of lessons about why and how companies pursue successful M&A strategies and shows how M&A permits renewal and adaptation to uncertain conditions. It is a must read for anyone involved in corporate development and, especially, for CEOs seeking ways to adapt and prosper in the present challenging economic environment."

—Enrique R. Arzac, professor of finance and economics, Columbia Business School

"I agree entirely with the central thesis of Merge Ahead: that companies need to think of acquisitions, alliances, and organic growth as coherent synergistic moves rather than isolated one-off activities. The authors also do a wonderful job of laying out the major developments that are reshaping the global competitive landscape and that will keep mergers and acquisitions as core to the agenda of most companies. I enjoyed reading the book and benefited from it. It is a must read for anybody who wants to understand how the ongoing developments in the global economy will reshape the future of M&A activity."

—Anil K. Gupta, Ralph J. Tyser Professor of Strategy and Organization, Smith Business School, The University of Maryland and author of Getting China and India Right

"In a very accessible way, Justin and Gerald provide practical and thoughtful ways to advance the art and science of mergers and acquisitions."

—Charles Simmons, vice pr
development, Bristol-My

D1372208

"The road ahead has never been less well marked, making success all the more rewarding for those who navigate well. Merge Ahead will keep you pointed in the right direction. Read this book and you won't forget where you are going or why you are going there."

—Lee Kaplan, senior vice president and chief administrative officer, Enterprise Rent-a-Car Company

"Merge Ahead provides a compelling and lucid case for "merganic growth"—integrated make, buy, and borrow capabilities—essential to companies that aspire to sustained, profitable growth in today's ultra-challenging world."

—M. Carl Johnson, III, senior vice president and chief strategy officer, Campbell's Soup Company

"Pettit and Adolph clearly understand that M&A, like any corporate investment, must be designed and executed to add value for shareholders. Merge Ahead shows how M&A can deliver such returns."

—Don Chew, editor, Journal of Applied Corporate Finance, Morgan Stanley

"Merge Ahead is an insightful look at the trends driving M&A strategy and practice and a reminder that successful M&A is an important tool to add to an organic growth strategy. In a time when getting M&A right is more important than ever, Adolph and Pettit clearly explain how to raise your game."

—Andrew Bonfield, chief financial officer, Cadbury plc

MERGE AHEAD

strategy+business

MERGE AHEAD

Mastering the Five Enduring Trends of Artful M&A

GERALD ADOLPH AND JUSTIN PETTIT WITH MICHAEL SISK

New York   Chicago   San Francisco   Lisbon   London
Madrid   Mexico City   Milan   New Delhi   San Juan
Seoul   Singapore   Sydney   Toronto

The **McGraw·Hill** Companies

booz&co.

Booz & Company is publisher of *strategy+business* magazine.

Copyright ©2009 by Booz & Company Inc. All rights reserved.
Printed in the United States of America. Except as permitted under
the United States Copyright Act of 1976, no part of this publication
may be reproduced or distributed in any form or by any means, or
stored in a data base or retrieval system, without the prior written
permission of the publisher.

1 2 3 4 5 6 7 8 9 0   DOC/DOC   0 1 3 2 1 0 9

ISBN 978-0-07-150832-2
MHID   0-07-150832-5

Design by Lee Fukui and Mauna Eichner

McGraw-Hill books are available at special quantity discounts to use
as premiums and sales promotions, or for use in corporate training
programs. To contact a representative, please visit the Contact Us
pages at www.mhprofessional.com.

To Leroy and Beryl for their love,
commitment, and sacrifice
G.A.

To Krista, Trevor, Madeleine, and
Teddy for their love and laughter
J.P.

CONTENTS

M&A'S MERGANIC FUTURE

PRECIOUS FEW companies outperform Warren Buffett's Berkshire Hathaway over the long term. But Danaher Corporation accomplished this feat for 15 years, between 1993 and 2008. Danaher is a $19 billion diversified industrial company, best known in the United States as the maker of Craftsman brand mechanics' tools for Sears. The company did this by expertly developing and executing three types of activities—mergers and acquisitions, organic growth, and alliances—as one synchronized growth strategy. Danaher's leaders are always exploring ways in which acquisitions, divestitures, new business development, marketing, innovation, licensing, joint ventures, and other collaborative alliances can be used, in an integrated fashion, to achieve its overall short- and long-term goals.

Most companies, of course, use all of these growth levers at one time or another. But few companies consciously use them in ways that consistently reinforce and build on each other's impact. Of course, Danaher is not always buying companies, forming alliances, and launching organic growth initiatives simultaneously. Corporate growth doesn't have to happen in such a literal-minded fashion to be effective. Rather, the idea is to keep these three growth avenues continually active and to deploy them as appropriate to make the most of varying market conditions. Any company with an effective growth strategy is always in some stage of merger and acquisition (M&A) preparation or action, is always assessing and executing alliances, *and* is always innovating and expanding its existing operations.

Many factors, including the Danaher Business System (an ingrained management approach based on lean production principles), may have helped the company thrive, but its skill at combining all three forms of growth is an undeniable asset. The most critical element is to keep all three levers tightly intertwined. That's what distinguishes an integrated growth strategy (or, as it will be called in this book, a "merganic" strategy—interrelating mergers and organic growth) from simply having three different ways to pursue a similar outcome. Just as this strategy has set Danaher apart from competitors, so has its performance. While the U.S. hand tools business declined overall between 1998 and 2008, Danaher achieved overall compound annual revenue growth of more than 15 percent. (Like most companies, Danaher suffered severe revenue drops in the fourth quarter of 2008; its growth rate shrank to 1.1 percent. And it has projected a 10 percent decline in annual earnings for 2009. But that still represents highly successful performance for that time frame.)

Other companies that have adopted integrated strategies to unlock their full potential include such prominent companies as General Electric (GE), HSBC, InBev, Johnson & Johnson (J&J), and Procter & Gamble (P&G). All of these companies are known in M&A circles for their tightly integrated use of M&A, organic growth, and alliances to drive above-average growth.

Mergers and acquisitions have been an important factor in corporate performance and strategy since the 1960s, and, as this book will demonstrate, their influence is going to remain strong in the future. But they will no longer be isolated events; M&A will be increasingly integrated into every major company's overall strategy for growth. Familiar types of M&A strategy, such as the approach taken by J&J and P&G to extend into adjacent products and services for new sources of revenue, are much more effective when combined with internal innovation initiatives (organic growth) and partnerships with other companies. (P&G is even known for its interest in alliances with competitors.)

The financial meltdown of autumn 2008 and its aftermath might seem to challenge the idea of integrated growth in general and mergers and acquisitions in particular. In early 2009, the global economy headed into an extended retrenchment, with tight credit, rising unemployment, a great deal of uncertainty, and a consensus that the recovery could be slow and prolonged. It is beyond the scope of this book, or any book, to predict the outcome in any detail. But the overall pattern is clear: corporate leaders will need to marshall their resources, focus their strategy, and build their growth capabilities—not just to survive the downturn but to emerge stronger.

All indications suggest that as these economic dynamics unfold, consolidation and alliances will be critical. And an integrated approach to growth may be the cornerstone of strategy for many successful companies. In this context, and also based on the history of past downturns, there is every reason to expect a favorable climate for mergers and acquisitions as the economy moves forward. The downward pressure on companies and the lowering of valuations will create attractive acquisition opportunities, and the demand for growth will spur companies to take advantage of them. Similarly, organic growth strategies, when managed effectively, executed frugally, and designed for increasingly cost-conscious consumers, will be more vital than ever. Finally, a downturn produces many new opportunities for alliances, with companies having a much better chance of surviving if they learn to work in tandem.

It is not unusual for many companies to exercise these three approaches. But the companies that are most likely to do well during this turbulent period, and to lead their industries when the recovery comes, are those that can put them together in an aligned, purposeful manner. Organic growth alone will not suffice to achieve above-average growth in the long term—M&A and alliances will be necessary. All three of them will need to be executed with vigor and in quantity; an integrated growth strategy means more than the odd acquisition or occasional alliance.

This book is called *Merge Ahead* because it explores the role of M&A in corporate growth. At any given moment, there is a merger or acquisition ahead in the future of most major companies. Prudent M&A is a powerful instrument of renewal and an essential way to remain flexible in the face of ever-changing industry and economic conditions.

Conventional wisdom might argue that in the past, M&A has destroyed value more often than it has created it; this view has understandably led some managers to avoid M&A altogether. But if you believe that organic growth is not enough, then the challenges of M&A must be mastered; and the rewards for success are worth the effort. The ultimate goal of this book is to better the odds of achieving successful, sustained results and to help executives think about deals in the context of the larger growth story. Indeed, when some of the deal-making principles advanced by Booz & Company—principles that we discuss in greater detail later in this book—are applied, the success rates of M&A dramatically improve.

The first step toward bettering the M&A odds is to develop a sound understanding of the forces shaping the context within which deals take place. By now, most executives are well aware that the events of the mid-2000s to the late 2000s—globalization, deregulation, technological advances, and, of course, the credit crisis of 2008/2009—have created a radically different business environment from that of the late 1990s. This environment is evolving with remarkable speed.

THE FIVE MOST CRITICAL TRENDS

The future of mergers and acquisitions will be shaped by five ongoing large-scale phenomena that directly influence the way deals will unfold. As with all long-term trends, the timing of particular events is unknown, and it's not clear exactly how they will unfold, but it is possible to look at the overall patterns and draw some reliable conclusions about their impact.

Here, then, are the driving forces we can identify with some confidence, no matter how the economic turbulence of 2008-2009 plays out. In general, the size of companies will continually increase, while scale and strategic focus will become more important. The velocity of capital, business, and information will accelerate, and investors and managers will be ever more impatient in seeking results. New competitors will continue to rise from emerging economies, with greater success and influence, especially in acquisitions and alliances. The influence of financial buyers will not disappear with the end of the credit bubble; however, the nature of its most active participants will change. And the economy will generate more frequent and more significant waves and bubbles.

Trend 1: Big Is Bigger Than Ever

As companies compete and seek the marketplace reach they need for viability, they will need to get bigger. Marketing, sales, supply chains, and service functions are being expanded and adapted to a host of geographic markets and adjacent segments and services. At the same time, many basic participation costs of doing business are escalating, which means that companies need greater investment capacity and financial muscle just to stay even or to thrive. For instance, new marketing technologies allow companies to create so-called segments of one to reach customers better, but these are expensive tools. A CEO and executive team might reasonably ask, "How big must we get to be able to afford these technologies?" and then pursue growth to attain that size. This imperative naturally makes mergers and acquisitions more appealing and has helped drive M&A activity.

However, big is often regarded as an undesirable corporate attribute. Citigroup's recent troubles, for example, are often pegged to its creation of a gigantic "financial supermarket." Witness also the language that is frequently used to describe big companies, such as "behemoth," "sprawling," and "lumbering."

But getting bigger in this emerging environment does not simply mean an increase in size. Coherence—the complexity, range, and related nature of a company's offerings—is an equally significant factor in a company's ability to sustain its competitiveness against rivals. Together, size and coherence create the *relevant* scale that helps companies gain the depth and expertise they need if they are to deploy their assets and capabilities (such as technologies, customers, and supply chains) effectively. This insight might seem simple, but it represents a critical evolution beyond the prevailing conglomerate mindset of the past 40 years—a mindset that formerly focused on size alone, with insufficient emphasis on coherence beyond a financial rationale.

Trend 2: Velocity and Impatience

Capital and information are moving in greater quantities and over greater distances more rapidly than ever—around the clock, across borders, and in real time—thanks to advances in technology and the global networking of media and markets. Customers shift their purchasing habits and investors shift their funds with unprecedented speed. With a few keystrokes, revenue and capital flow into and out of industries and companies.

Along with this velocity has come a cultural impatience among all of a company's stakeholders, including its investors, business partners, customers, and employees. Investors demand returns; business partners don't tolerate delays; customers expect prompt service; talented employees expect instantaneous rewards and quick promotions.

The consequence of all this velocity and impatience is an anxious, high-strung mindset that now defines the way the world's major physical and financial markets view corporate performance. Minuscule time delays and tiny price differentials can quickly translate into huge losses from defecting investors, business partners, customers, or employees, upping the ante on even the slightest corporate delay or misstep. This "side effect" of velocity, of course, was one of the factors contributing to the financial "tsunami" (as some have called it) of 2008 and 2009. But the factors leading to it will not go away as the economy shifts; no matter how long the downturn lasts, the increase in velocity and impatience will remain.

This creates extraordinary pressure on corporate leaders to execute complex deal strategies instantaneously, and without a hiccup, once they are ready to go forward. The conundrum for managers is that in reality, big, complex mergers and acquisitions should not be undertaken at high speed. They can take many months, if not years, to evaluate, negotiate, and integrate fully. Yet stakeholders now want positive results from every deal in short order. Corporate leaders will increasingly be judged on their ability to satisfy the seemingly incompatible needs for speed and deal quality.

Trend 3: The New Blues

Globalization has created a raft of new opportunities for companies and state-owned businesses in emerging markets to compete, relatively unhindered by the intense regulation, trade barriers, vying political ideologies, and antagonism toward capitalism that hobbled them in the recent past. Companies emerging from nations such as Brazil, Russia, India, Saudi Arabia, and China are competing head to head with the most renowned blue chip companies from North America, Europe, and Japan—and they are competing not just locally, but globally. Call these recent entrants the "New Blue Chips." In their home nations, fast-emerging middle classes will continue to develop—perhaps not as rapidly as they did in the mid-2000s, but at least rapidly enough to support high-growth, influential new world-class companies.

The New Blues are especially adept at serving developing nations, but they will also compete in providing products and services for developed nations. The New Blues have seasoned management teams with international experience at leading companies, and they will continue to change the face of M&A globally as they compete for deals and collectively form a new pool of potential partners. Furthermore, the New Blues are remaking their industries through domestic and regional acquisitions, and they have set their sights on developed markets and the companies headquartered within them. Saudi Basic Industries, for instance, paid $11.6 billion for GE Plastics in 2007, and in early 2008, Tata Motors purchased the storied Jaguar and Land Rover brands from Ford for $2.3 billion. Tata said that Ford will continue to supply engines, transmissions, and other components for five to nine years, ironically turning one of America's Big Three into a tier 1 supplier for an Indian automaker!

Trend 4: Deep Pockets

In addition to the New Blues, another set of powerful new competitors has emerged: financial buyers in the form of private equity funds, hedge funds, infrastructure funds, and sovereign wealth funds. Until the credit crisis, many of these funds were able to tap into enormous and fast-growing pools of capital from institutional investors, governments, and wealthy individuals around the globe. Though the sources of capital may be different as the downturn continues to unfold, the availability of capital for M&A will continue. There is a lot of investment capital left in the system that is still looking for returns. Some have compared it to a lake of capital, caught behind a dam of mistrust and fear. But sooner or later, as the economy earns back the confidence of investors, capital will flow again.

For private equity funds in particular, given their historical preference for traditional M&A—taking controlling stakes in companies—rather than the minority positions preferred by sovereign wealth funds and hedge funds, access to capital gave them the ability to spend vast sums to acquire companies. Along with this financial clout came a willingness to invest in and strategically reposition acquisitions before reselling them, often taking three to five years, and sometimes more, to do so.

This newfound patience is partly born of necessity. A rising number of bidders for deals means higher purchase prices, requiring more work and the time to realize the gains. After the credit bubble collapsed, private equity had to invest more capital in deals and faced more challenging exit scenarios—another factor demanding time. Private equity firms that have survived the credit collapse shakeout have had to learn to play the game of patient capital, cultivating a success rate that is high enough that as their early efforts pay off, those wins can fund their later endeavors. While these private equity firms are still driven to wring out cost savings as aggressively as possible, the old "strip and flip" game of selling off parts of the business, slashing jobs, and reselling the company in a year or two is increasingly seen as counterproductive—even in the short run. Thus, like the New Blues, private equity has emerged as a direct competitor to established strategic buyers in the M&A marketplace. And, although the credit crisis has dramatically dampened its influence, as liquidity returns to the capital markets, private equity's M&A activities will resume and, indeed, increase.

Other financial players, especially sovereign wealth funds, family trusts, and government investment funds, are also shifting their focus to more strategic investment, away from reliance on financial managers with short-term portfolios. This adds one more group of active players to the M&A market, either as partners with or as competitors to strategic buyers.

Trend 5: Bubbles and Waves

The first four trends—the need to get bigger and more coherent; the need to respond rapidly to impatient capital, high-velocity information, and expectations; and the stepped-up competition from New Blues and private equity buyers—have spawned periods of industry consolidation that are occurring with greater frequency and volume. This manifests itself in two recurring economic phenomena: waves and bubbles.

Waves and bubbles are interrelated; both are reflected in the volatility of corporate deal making and in acquisition price fluctuation. But they are two different types of phenomena. Waves represent medium- to long-term structural changes in an industry. In recent years, waves of consolidation caused by technology breakthroughs and deregulation have occurred in the biotech, banking, and telecom industries. Bubbles are more speculative; they represent temporary anomalies in the market, driven by changes in sentiment and short-term supply-and-demand imbalances. They are also more disruptive, overinflating valuations, making it difficult for buyers to craft sound offers, and creating havoc when they pop. The momentum of capital, more than fundamental industry change, drives consolidation bubbles.

Maintaining business vitality through waves and bubbles, with disciplined risk management, is a major challenge for companies in today's business environment. The ability to consciously manage these forces, avoiding underinvestment at the bottom of a business cycle and overpaying at its peak, will distinguish the most effective companies from their competitors.

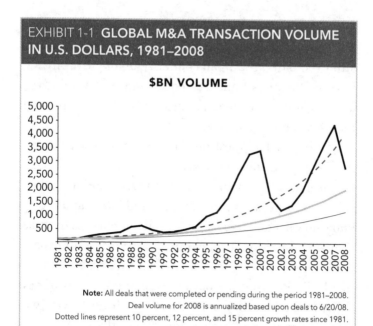

EXHIBIT 1-1 **GLOBAL M&A TRANSACTION VOLUME IN U.S. DOLLARS, 1981–2008**

$BN VOLUME

Note: All deals that were completed or pending during the period 1981–2008.
Deal volume for 2008 is annualized based upon deals to 6/20/08.
Dotted lines represent 10 percent, 12 percent, and 15 percent growth rates since 1981.

Source: Thomson Banker

RAISING THE ODDS OF SUCCESS

The five trends, when considered together, have two broad implications. First, they explain the burgeoning growth in M&A activity. Exhibit 1-1 shows that global M&A activity has grown from $92.1 billion in 1981 to $4.4 trillion in 2007, and all indications are that the long-term trend line will continue to rise.

Of course, the long-term increase in M&A activity has been interrupted at times. M&A volume often rises and falls in response to global economic conditions, and in late 2008 this volume crashed, along with most other financial indicators, in response to frozen credit markets and global recession. But even accounting for down years, and despite great volatility, the long-term global activity trend line continues to point upward. Because strong companies still exist, still seeking to capitalize on opportunities to improve their positions created by reduced corporate valuations, one can expect that growth to continue through recession and turbulence.

The second implication of the five trends is the urgent need for more effective M&A practice—in terms of strategy, deal making, integration planning, execution, and results. No corporate strategist can avoid M&A, and yet few know how to conduct M&A with reliable success in situation after situation, expansion opportunity after expansion opportunity. That's a serious failing. Executives involved in M&A these days must bring a variety of new skills to the job: they must choose their deals wisely to achieve size and depth; they must fortify their M&A practice in response to the velocity and impatience of markets; they must respond quickly to competitive challenges and partnering opportunities from the New Blues and private equity investors, acting and reacting to capture M&A opportunities as soon as they arise; and they must navigate fast-paced cycles, understanding how to tell the difference between a wave and a bubble and how to pursue deals in either environment.

Attaining this level of proficiency is no small challenge for many companies. In one study, illustrated in Exhibit 1-2, Booz & Company analyzed M&A transactions over a 10-year period from 1995 to 2005. It turned out that nearly one-half (49 percent) of all companies that made deals valued at $100 million or more experienced declines in excess shareholder value in the two-year postdeal period. Moreover, about two-thirds of the companies were

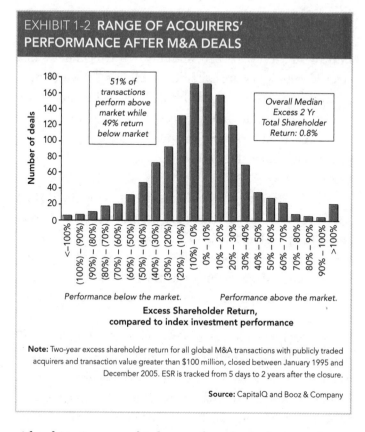

EXHIBIT 1-2 **RANGE OF ACQUIRERS' PERFORMANCE AFTER M&A DEALS**

51% of transactions perform above market while 49% return below market

Overall Median Excess 2 Yr Total Shareholder Return: 0.8%

Performance below the market.   *Performance above the market.*

Excess Shareholder Return, compared to index investment performance

Note: Two-year excess shareholder return for all global M&A transactions with publicly traded acquirers and transaction value greater than $100 million, closed between January 1995 and December 2005. ESR is tracked from 5 days to 2 years after the closure.

Source: CapitalQ and Booz & Company

either big winners or big losers: they showed excess share-holder return of either more than a positive 20 percent or more than a negative 20 percent during the first two years after the deal.

When these merger failures are analyzed, execution problems (rather than strategic missteps) account for two-thirds of the failures. Problems with execution might include weak due diligence, lack of accountability for various aspects of the deal and postmerger integration, culture clash between the companies, loss of key staff and customers, and poor external communications.

If there is a silver lining to this unsettling track record, it's that merger and acquisition strategy and execution are improving. Ten years ago, about two-thirds of deals destroyed value and were considered failures, far worse than today's 50/50 outcome. Still, that leaves a lot of deals on the scrap heap, a lot of executives out of jobs, and a lot of angry shareholders. And the odds of success won't improve much more if the old ways of conducting M&A continue.

Clearly, Herodotus could have been talking about M&A when he said, "Great deeds are usually wrought at great risk." The problem is that too many companies pay too little attention to the complexities that give rise to the risk. When companies master the critical factors that can lead to success, they operate with a more consistent track record.

The proper approach to M&A, as detailed in Chapter 7 of this book, begins with a corporate growth plan, based on a capabilities-based road map to help envision where the business wants to go, what capabilities it must accrue, and in what order it must accrue them. Over time, this "capability chaining" approach will synchronize M&A along with alliances and organic growth in a multifaceted and integrated plan that is the heart of a merganic strategy.

THE MERGANIC STRATEGY

The Danaher Corporation's story, during its 15-year growth period, provides a case study of effective growth. The company's focus on organic measures netted a respectable 4 to 6 percent annual growth rate. But to reach 15.4 percent

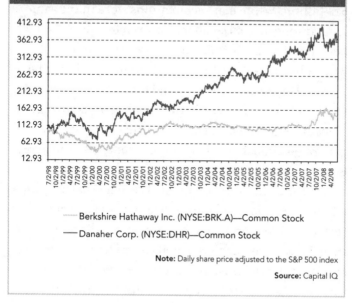

EXHIBIT 1-3 **RELATIVE SHARE PRICES OF DANAHER AND BERKSHIRE HATHAWAY, DAILY PRICES ADJUSTED FOR S&P 500 INDEX, 1998–2008**

------- Berkshire Hathaway Inc. (NYSE:BRK.A)—Common Stock

——— Danaher Corp. (NYSE:DHR)—Common Stock

Note: Daily share price adjusted to the S&P 500 index

Source: Capital IQ

growth overall, the company had to work the other two growth levers pretty hard. Our shorthand name "merganic" (after the mergers and organic growth that form its most visible components) refers to this kind of combined approach: mergers, alliances, and organic growth tightly joined in pursuing the same goals with complementary capabilities. This is not old-style conglomerate building.

Consider the details of Danaher's merganic strategy. This will help explain how the tool company regularly outperformed Berkshire Hathaway, let alone the S&P 500, as shown in Exhibit 1-3.

On the M&A front, Danaher used an active portfolio approach to M&A that balanced divestitures, "bolt-on" acquisitions, and "new platform" acquisitions. The company's M&A activity between 1998 and 2008 included more than 60 acquisitions and divestitures, totaling about $12 billion. While most acquisitions were in the same or similar industries, Danaher also stretched into new markets. But not any "attractive" market; it targeted markets with substantive capability linkages to its existing businesses. For instance, as the hand tools business declined along with Sears's fortunes, Danaher began acquiring a set of medical instruments companies that by the end of 2005 generated almost one-half of the company's annual revenues.

Danaher also actively pursued strategic partnerships, alliances, and joint ventures—business deals that created *virtual scale* and provided the company with greater clout than it could have achieved on its own. Virtual scale is essentially any business collaboration—formal or informal—that attempts to pool assets, capabilities, and/or costs to achieve some of the same benefits of relevant scale that might be achieved through acquisitions or sustained organic growth. One example is the alliance of Danaher subsidiary Leica Microsystems with Veeco Instruments. In 2007, Leica and Veeco announced a collaboration to serve the nascent field of nanomedicine that combined Leica's ability to measure biological samples with Veeco's high-resolution molecular imaging technology. The combination enabled the companies to quickly introduce innovative research instruments that enjoy a competitive advantage in the marketplace.

Does every company on earth need to shift gears and adopt a merganic strategy? Some argue that a company that excels at organic growth need not worry about mergers, acquisitions, or alliances. While the relative mix of M&A, organic growth, and virtual scale is unique for every company and changes with economic conditions and stage in a business's life cycle, even the most successful organically driven companies of our era have also paid close attention to all three forms of growth.

Take Toyota, a company that has perhaps the world's greatest track record for organic growth, with the size, success, and culture of innovation to match. Toyota is notably conservative and very deliberate when it comes to M&A, but nevertheless, it does pursue deals. In 2000, for example, Toyota Industries acquired BT Industries, extending its line of lift trucks and expanding its share of the global market to 25 percent. In 2005, Toyota Motor bought GM's stake in Subaru parent Fuji Heavy Industries. In April 2008, Toyota announced that it would almost double that stake to 16.5 percent and also pursue virtual scale by establishing a vehicle development partnership with Subaru and Daihatsu, a Toyota subsidiary acquired in 1998.

Toyota's story demonstrates that even those organizations that are the very best at organic growth dare not rely entirely on their existing operations to sustain above-average results. In the long run, it's difficult for any company to outperform the average growth in its industry. Indeed, most companies in most industries are faced with the ongoing dilemma of declining organic growth.

Many studies have shown how hard it is to maintain adequate performance through organic growth alone. Even highly valued companies must maintain their reputation with investors by generating consistent returns greater than their current cost of capital and growth that is superior to that of their peers. That's no small task, and, as executives well know, growth can actually destroy value if the incremental earnings it generates are less than the cost of the capital it requires. In short, it takes a good deal of profitable growth to get best-in-class valuations.

Most executives know that they cannot lean too heavily on organic growth alone for above-average growth. But in many cases they are still uneasy pursuing M&A and alliances—understandably, given the current risks and historically poor outcome of many M&A deals and collaborations. In contrast, some executives turn to M&A too quickly, seeing it as a panacea for any shortfall in internal growth. The value of merganic growth is that by intertwining all three levers of growth in pursuit of an overall expansion and development strategy, executives can balance risks while ensuring continuous renewal. That, in itself, makes growth in the long run more feasible.

While the argument for merganic growth is compelling, achieving it is inherently difficult. Making it work requires a variety of skills and capabilities, ranging from the deep market insight and foresight needed to get beyond the obvious to financial acumen to the ability to manage postmerger integration and human capital issues on a global scale. For most companies, the most difficult impediment will not be the outside world, but their own internal limits: the need to build the skills and capabilities necessary for merganic growth, and to adopt the strategies and tactics required to execute it.

Of course, even a great merganic growth strategy will fail if the individual transactions are not executed well. In addition to having a merganic strategy, executives must master the art and science of M&A execution, and successfully apply it to each individual deal that they undertake.

The successful execution of M&A transactions, as we discuss in Chapter 8, is dependent on an efficient, comprehensive process of deal design, negotiation, and execution. Any individual M&A deal has four distinct stages. First, the predeal business case must be crafted. Building an "enhanced" business case in this stage plays a more crucial role than ever before. Using the merganic road map, it fosters enough early preparation that later stages will be robust despite the increasing velocity with which they will need to be conducted. This first stage is also the point where corporate leaders distinguish those elements of a deal over which they have little or no control (inherent elements) and those elements in which they can affect outcomes (action elements). Both types of elements are present in every deal, but unless leaders recognize and plan for the differences between the two, the risk of a failed deal increases.

The second stage is the actual deal making, which includes the offer, negotiation, financing, and a new type of due diligence: strategic due diligence. This represents the validation of the enhanced business case through in-depth exploration of the fit between the two merging companies.

The third stage is the design of the new company and planning of the integration process using best practices and ingrained expertise to avoid the pitfalls that have scuttled many other deals.

Fourth is the execution, which begins with the closing of the deal and requires a concerted level of discipline to deliver the plan while avoiding drift.

To improve the likelihood of M&A success, executives must prepare all of these elements in advance and design the linkages among them. Unfortunately, these four stages are often treated as a series of "batonlike" handoffs: from boardrooms to deal makers to integration planning program offices to operational managers. By contrast, the most successful companies will employ a more holistic approach in which aspects of all four stages are pursued concurrently, either by the same people or by a closely knit team of people who communicate easily and regularly with one another.

MERGE AHEAD

Though M&A success is an artful process that follows no universal "scientific" formula, it need not be a spin of the roulette wheel. In fact, sound M&A practices can be replicated and learned. This is evident in the track record of such "serial acquirers" as Cisco Systems, Danaher, GE, HSBC, and Johnson & Johnson. Their experiences show that systematic success is possible if senior managers have the right experience and mindset, and if they position their companies—culturally, structurally, and technologically—to seek out acquisitions and integrate them with current operations.

One final factor—the nature of competition itself—suggests that corporate leaders will continue to gain skill and confidence in the practice of M&A. This means that the pace and quality of M&A deal making will continue to increase. In his 2008 book *The Red Queen among Organizations: How Competitiveness Evolves*, Stanford University professor William P. Barnett proposes that continued competition leads to increased pressure in a never-ending cycle. "Organizations learn in response to competition, making them stronger competitors and so triggering learning in their rivals," he writes. Something very similar is happening in the world of mergers and acquisitions—indeed, in all of the components of merganic growth. The more proficient companies get, the more intensely they match their rivals and partners, and the faster the process becomes. Thus, if companies were traveling on the M&A highway at 40 miles per hour a few years ago, they are now traveling at 80 miles per hour. It's a dangerous situation for the unpracticed: a jerk of the wheel that might once have caused a brief swerve now can put the deal in a ditch.

The objective of this book is to smooth the ride. By studying the five trends shaping the future of M&A specifically, understanding how M&A fits into the merganic growth strategy, and skillfully managing the life cycle of their deals, corporate leaders can better understand the nature and implications of the evolving business environment, and thus be better positioned to execute deals and deliver the targeted results.

So, keep both hands on the wheel; there's a merge ahead.

2

BIG IS BIGGER
THAN EVER

THE FINANCIAL HEADLINES provide ample proof that "big" is bigger than ever in the world of business. French utilities Gaz de France and Suez pursue a $107 billion merger that would create the world's third-largest power-generating company (Exhibit 2-1 shows CEOs Gerard Mestrallet of Suez and Jean-François Cirelli of Gaz de France shaking hands during the negotiations; it had taken them 18 months to gain the support of key shareholders). Belgium's InBev bought U.S.-based Anheuser-Busch for $52 billion, the largest cash deal in history, further solidifying InBev's position as the world's largest brewer. Wells Fargo bought distressed Wachovia for $12.7 billion, creating the second-largest U.S. bank. And, in January 2009, despite the credit and economic crisis, the world's largest drug maker, Pfizer, announced plans to get bigger yet by acquiring Wyeth for $68 billion.

EXHIBIT 2-1 **CEOS GERARD MESTRALLET OF SUEZ AND JEAN-FRANÇOIS CIRELLI OF GAZ DE FRANCE**

Source: Benoit Tessier/Reuters

Stories like this will continue to appear, no matter how the global recession unfolds, as companies in virtually every industry strive to compete in a more global, more consolidated, more competitive environment. From Beijing to São Paolo, from London to New York, from Dubai to Mumbai, greater competition and greater opportunities—locally, regionally, and internationally—brought on by customer demands, deregulation, and technology advances will continue to force corporate leaders to think about expansion. They will recognize that the largest companies have an edge in most business environments: in their ability to deploy resources, enter markets, and (for many companies) raise capital.

The general advantages of size are so well recognized that they have become an ongoing influence on prevailing attitudes about corporate strategy, and about mergers and acquisitions in particular. The inflated price tags of deals during the mid-2000s obscures the real trend, a trend toward larger and larger companies.

But "big" doesn't mean what it used to mean. Today's biggest companies are not lumbering, inflexible conglomerates. Successful players are empowered, rather than hobbled, by their size; they can grow without being nearly as bureaucratic as the giant hierarchies of, say, the 1960s and 1970s. This is because of a shift in the prevailing understanding of "big," especially with regard to corporate strategy and M&A. Today, the critical aspect of bigness is the scale of a company and the flexibility that this scale brings, not the company's size per se. The ability to gain the advantages of *relevant* scale, as opposed to just the benefits of size, will make all the difference in the effectiveness of corporate activity and will define the gap between winners and losers in the future.

TOO BIG TO FAIL

The late 2008 adoption of government intervention policies in the United States and the United Kingdom, in which many companies are seen as "too big to fail," provides a telling indicator of how big "big" has become in the business world. In a backhanded way, it also suggests that bigness confers another advantage: a societal safety net that protects the largest companies from the worst consequences of business failure.

Historically, the concept of too-big-to-fail (TBTF) was applied only to banks. TBTF emerged as a U.S. government policy in 1984, after the asset base of

Continental Illinois National Bank and Trust Company, the nation's seventh-largest bank, was decimated by a rout in the energy sector. Subsequently, a depositor run brought the bank to the edge of insolvency. After initial attempts to prop up the bank failed, the Federal Deposit Insurance Corporation (FDIC) took over the bank, buying its worst assets and providing liquidity. In the Senate hearings that followed, the comptroller of the currency stated that the U.S. government would not let any of the nation's 11 largest banks fail. This established the TBTF principle. Outside the United States, some national industries, such as airlines, were also viewed as too strategically important to be left to the whims of the market.

As the world's economy crashed in 2008, TBTF was not only applied to the banking industry but expanded to other U.S. sectors. Other countries put in place similar policies, all recognizing, in effect, that a sudden major corporate collapse could produce rapid, dangerous effects on the rest of the economy. In the United Kingdom, the government intervened to support Royal Bank of Scotland. In the United States, the insurance company AIG, which was the eighteenth-largest company in the world, received an initial $85 billion credit infusion (followed by additional support) from the government. The rationale was simply the draconian effects that AIG's failure would have on companies and markets around the world. And as General Motors approached bankruptcy, the government stepped in with a loan of

$13.4 billion under the Troubled Assets Relief Program (TARP)—to protect not just GM but also its suppliers and dealers and the communities in which its employees lived. This bailout even had the support of competitors; they also relied on GM's vast network of suppliers, and they feared adverse consequences for their own supplies if GM failed.

Opposition to TBTF stems from the concept of "moral hazard." When institutions are protected by the government from the consequences of their actions, they will take on greater risk than they should and let others bear the costs of their failures or problems. It is too soon to tell how long government-sponsored TBTF-style "bailouts" will endure, or whether the spread of TBTF mentality will spur a new wave of consolidation. But one aspect of their future is certain: the debate over which companies deserve such interventions will continue. The most common criteria for bailouts will be the new definition of bigness of the companies and the perceived impact of their demise. The TBTF approach may not protect all large companies in the future, but it will tend to ensure that when large companies die, it will happen through acquisition, divestiture, and slow erosion, not through sudden collapse.

A NEW DEFINITION OF SCALE: COHERENCE

The traditional concept of economies of scale goes back to the nineteenth-century economist Alfred Marshall;

economic historian Alfred D. Chandler, Jr., articulated it in modern terms in his 1990 book *Scale and Scope: The Dynamics of Industrial Capitalism*. The size of a company can be measured in assets, market value of shares, or the size of the workforce, Chandler wrote, but "statistics cannot convey either the complexity or the nature and functions of [a company]." Rather, scale is represented by the company's output: the range of products and services it offers, the regions and territories and customer groups that it serves, and the costs at which it can provide its wares. One indicator of a company's breadth is the number of strategic business units (or, as Chandler called them, "operating units") that it has and the productivity of those businesses. A company's scale increases when its business units increase in size and capability, with the effect of enabling that company to offer more products and services, in more markets, at lower sustained costs.

Traditional cost-oriented scale by itself may not be sufficient for a company to succeed today, or in the future. A more appropriate prerequisite would be *relevant* scale, or coherence: the level of overall coordination and mutual reinforcement among a company's capabilities and assets that helps its businesses grow, compete, or achieve superior profitability. Without this coordination, economies of scale and competitive advantage are diminished. For example, acquiring a local manufacturing company based in Cape Town may not provide relevant scale for a conglomerate with interests in emerging markets if that is its only business in southern Africa. But the same manufacturing acquisition might be a terrific match, in terms of relevant scale, for a company with a string of related business interests in the region. Having scale in purchasing isn't relevant if a company simply buys more supplies from more purveyors, but it's very relevant if it reduces costs or improves viability for suppliers—and therefore offers a customer with relevant scale more bargaining power. A smaller company with a coherent portfolio might have more of this relevant scale than a larger, more diverse company.

Scale, when it is relevant, provides the ability to operate more efficiently and effectively, mitigating risk with a strong balance sheet and operational flexibility in the process. Companies that achieve relevant scale gain the kind of leverage—the ability to generate greater results from the same investment—that is inherent in strong balance sheets. This enhanced flexibility enables companies to serve customers more effectively, creating solutions to their problems rather than simply selling them products. In all of these endeavors, size alone is not enough; some companies slow down and become less competitive as they get bigger. They gain size, but lose scale.

Gaining relevant scale is the critical enabler that allows a company to meet the three most critical challenges of today's business environment: *managing global differences* across a greater and more diverse set of markets; building a more profitable, loyal *customer base;* and wielding increased *financial muscle.* Let's look at each of these three challenges, and the way each affects the need for relevant scale, in more detail.

MANAGING GLOBAL DIFFERENCES

To the casual observer, the most visible driving factors in strategic M&A activity these days, aside from industry consolidation, would seem to be globalization. As *New York Times* foreign affairs columnist Thomas Friedman proclaimed in his bestselling 2005 book *The World Is Flat*, companies that were once barricaded behind national borders are now far more exposed to both opportunities (in the form of new markets) and threats (in the form of new competitors) from across the globe.

Certainly, cross-border mergers and acquisitions have become commonplace. Spain's Banco Santander owns the U.K.-based bank Abbey. German automaker Volkswagen owns Lamborghini (Italy), Skoda (Czech Republic), a controlling interest in Scania (Sweden), and Bentley (United Kingdom). Former national airlines KLM (Netherlands) and Air France are now joined in one holding company, Air France-KLM, which also owns CityJet (Ireland) and VLM (Finland). The Indian IT services provider Wipro Technologies owns the U.S. IT services provider Infocrossing. Some sectors, such as electric power and telecommunications, that were once seen as resolutely local are now expanding across national borders through M&A.

All together, between 2006 and 2007, the value of cross-border M&A transactions increased by 68 percent to $1.4 trillion, and the number of those transactions increased by 29 percent to 8,962. Firms from some regions, such as the Middle East, have only begun to demonstrate their interest in global M&A. As Exhibit 2-2 shows, there were at least 17 multibillion-dollar deals between 2005 and 2007 in which Middle East companies acquired companies in North America, Europe, Asia, and Australia. (An eighteenth deal, the bid by Delta Two of Qatar for the U.K. supermarket chain Sainsbury's, was never completed.) In some cases, the 2008-2009 recession created

EXHIBIT 2-2 MIDDLE EAST BUSINESSES GO GLOBAL: $1 BILLION+ ACQUISITIONS, 2005–2007

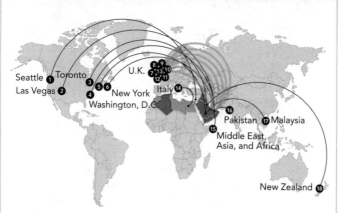

1. M1 Group (Lebanon) acquires Faconnable apparel line for $210 million, 2007.
2. Dubai World to invest $5.2 billion in MGM Mirage hotel and casino, 2007.
3. Kingdom Holding (Saudi Arabia) with Bill Gates acquires the Four Seasons hotel chain for $3.8 billion, 2007.
4. Mubadala (Abu Dhabi) buys 7.5 percent stake (worth $1.35 billion) in Carlyle Group, 2007.
5. Saudi Basic Industries Corporation acquires GE Plastics for $11.6 billion, 2007.
6. Istithmar (UAE) acquires Barneys luxury department store for $942 million, 2007.
7. Mumtalakat (Bahrain) acquires 30 percent of McLaren Group, 2007.
8. Qatar Investment Authority acquires 20 percent of the London Stock Exchange for $1.2 billion, 2007.
9. Dubai International Capital (UAE) acquires the Tussauds Group for around $1.5 billion, March 2005.
10. Dubai International Capital acquires Doncasters Group for $1.2 billion, 2006.
11. Dubai Ports World acquires the port operations company P&O for $9.2 billion, 2006.
12. Investment Dar (Kuwait) acquires Aston Martin for $925 million, 2007.
13. Delta Two (Qatar) bids for $1.5 billion of Sainsbury Stock, 2007.
14. Weather Investment (Egypt) acquires Wind in Italy for around $15 billion, 2005.
15. Etisalat (UAE) invests more than $8 billion since 2004 for expansion in the Middle East, Asia, and Africa.
16. Abu Dhabi IPIC plans $5 billion refinery in Pakistan, 2007.
17. Saudi Telecom buys 25 percent of Binariang, parent of Maxis, for $3.1 billion, 2007.
18. Agility (Kuwait) acquires LEP International, 2007.

Note: Transactions are noted as of January 1, 2008.

Source: Booz & Company

EXHIBIT 2-3 **CROSS-BORDER M&A, 1987–2007**

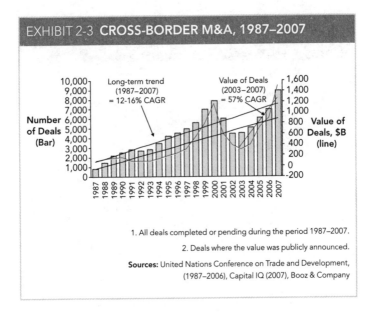

1. All deals completed or pending during the period 1987–2007.

2. Deals where the value was publicly announced.

Sources: United Nations Conference on Trade and Development, (1987–2006), Capital IQ (2007), Booz & Company

even greater interest in cross-border M&A. Chinese companies, for instance, began looking at the drop in the valuation of companies that provide strategic resources—such as oil, uranium, iron, lead, and tin—as opportunities to secure a stable flow of raw material via acquisition. Japanese companies have also found new cross-border buying opportunities in the recession; in 2008, according to Dealogic, they spent $77.8 billion on cross-border M&A, more than triple the 2007 total.

The overall trend of the past 20 years, as shown in Exhibit 2-3, suggests that, while there are always peaks and valleys, the overall number and size of cross-border deals will continue to increase. Indeed, since 1987, the volume and combined valuation of these deals have increased at a compound annual growth rate of between 12 and 16 percent. In 2007, cross-border deals exceeded the previous peak of 2000.

Do these transborder transactions meet the test of coherence and relevant scale? It would be oversimplistic to conclude that the world is fully flat—that global deals are easy now, or that national boundaries present no barriers. We agree with Pankaj Ghemawat, the IESE professor and author of *Redefining Global Strategy: Crossing Borders in a World Where Differences Still Matter*. As Ghemawat put it, "Levels of cross-border integration are currently increasing. They're even setting new records in some cases. But they still account for only a fraction of economic activity. Instead of being global, most companies that succeed are highly regional: They expand only to the markets where they can navigate the distances."

To Ghemawat, today's business environment is in a state of "semiglobalization," a very different phenomenon from full global interdependence. Our semiglobal world is not a fully integrated multinational environment; it features many cultural, administrative, geographic, and economic "distances" (as Ghemawat calls them) among nations. These barriers range from languages to the costs of transportation to the location of ports to the competitive boundaries set by existing businesses in each country. These are among factors that determine, for any given company, which types of cross-border expansion will be feasible and which will not.

Globalization has not paved over the unique qualities of national policies, cultures, customer preferences, currencies, and business standards and practices; it has connected them, creating economic superhighways—but with speed bumps. China and Brazil, for example, are usually regarded as indispensable for multinationals to enter. Both countries have large, growing economies and fast-emerging middle classes. But few companies would be foolish enough to manage their businesses and market their products and services in both of those countries in the same way—and the tactics for India, Russia, Vietnam, Egypt, and South Africa (to name just a few popular expansion targets) would also be different. One size does not fit all in the semiglobal world; the consumers of each nation demand products and services that are tailored to their distinctive needs and desires.

Why, then, with all its ambiguities and uncertainties, would this semiglobalization result in a trend toward bigger and more coherent companies? Some companies, such as healthcare providers and local utilities, might be perfectly happy to remain within their home region or nation. But many others must conduct business globally to deliver the growth rates their owners and investors demand, to follow their customers, or to respond to competitive threats. These companies are forced to expand across borders as they seek to satisfy their need to grow. They recognize that, in a semiglobal world, only businesses with relevant scale can afford to enter and compete in many different markets effectively.

In the next decade, as companies find themselves operating in more and more countries, they will need to find ways to add value while facing the myriad differences among these countries. Their marketing, sales, supply chains, and service functions will have to adapt to a host of geographic markets. They will need regulatory and operational acumen to reach into a variety of local markets deeply and efficiently, outmaneuvering rivals who lack the expertise to do so. Only companies with size can build the experiences and assets necessary to be profitable and to compete with small, local niche businesses. Building global capabilities—such as R&D in pharmaceuticals, drive trains in automotive, product platforms in consumer products, and operations expertise in utilities—gives companies the value across businesses that niche players cannot replicate. They can compete in multiple markets while enjoying the benefits of size. Relevant scale is a requirement for successful, economically viable semiglobalization.

Companies that navigate the transition to semiglobal scale have a dramatic edge over their rivals. For example, in the United States, tax codes, accounting rules, and terror prevention regulations enacted after September 11, 2001, have created a complicated operating environment for banks. For foreign banks looking to enter the U.S. banking market, this environment can seem daunting. Yet once established in the United States, some foreign banks, such as HSBC, Royal Bank of Canada (through its RBC Centura banks), and Royal Bank of Scotland (through Citizens Financial Group), have a significant deal-making advantage over other non-U.S. banks that lack the same experience and expertise.

BUILDING A CUSTOMER BASE

Another force driving companies to seek relevant scale is the increasingly varied nature of the consumer. Today, many companies are attempting to treat each customer as a so-called segment of one, providing individualized attention and individually tailored products and services. The added complexity of these customized services multiplies the challenges of semiglobalization a thousandfold. This is further complicated by the demands for local customization—personal tailoring of products and services—in the many consumer markets of our semiglobal environment.

To woo diverse customers in a digital era, many companies have invested in new marketing technologies. For instance, customer relationship management (CRM) software allows companies to create highly targeted outreach approaches that single out customers with near-personalized messages. But these are expensive tools. Making them economical often requires a greater size and market reach than many companies currently have, at least on their own.

Furthermore, once a customer has made a purchase, companies are increasingly seeking to leverage that new relationship for all it's worth by creating adjacent services and products. The alternative is to lose that hard-won customer over time or to be constantly locked in expensive share-shifting wars. To retain and hopefully grow their wallet share, companies must anticipate the new products and services that current customers will want and upgrade their offerings to meet that future demand.

This often means pushing beyond the boundaries of traditional market planning. For example, the telephone and cable companies over the past 10 years have evolved their offerings repeatedly to keep their customers, moving from providing simple cable TV or telephone service to embracing video-style playback and recording and packages combining video, voice, and data service. In the process, they have redefined their offerings in ways that create more revenue per consumer. Local "mom and pop" telephone or cable companies, or Internet service providers, could never compete at that scale.

Another classic example is the creation of PepsiCo in 1965 from the merger of Pepsi-Cola and Frito-Lay. Soft drinks and snack foods (enabled by direct store-delivery expertise in both businesses) turned out to be a perfect marketing match, and expanded Pepsi's customer wallet share. Five decades later, the deal remains an excellent example of relevant scale.

WIELDING
FINANCIAL MUSCLE

Companies need to compete effectively in a semiglobal environment, to serve ever more fragmented and diverse customer bases, and to capture more wallet share with broader and more sophisticated offerings—all of which cost money! The overall costs of doing business continue to escalate. Whether the expense is related to talent, research and development, transportation, information technology, or raw materials, investment requirements are expected to rise continuously over time. This, in turn, means that companies need greater investment capacity; they need to attract and deploy capital more flexibly and in larger amounts than ever before. This drives companies to strive for relevant scale.

Consider the capital required to establish and manage a global research and development footprint. According to an annual Booz & Company survey of innovation spending among the 1,000 largest public corporations worldwide, the share of R&D facilities located outside the home markets of multinational corporations has been rising steadily since 1975, and especially since 2005.

This shift is occurring for several reasons. Sometimes, companies are seeking to locate their R&D efforts close to their customers. In other instances, they are seeking cost advantages. In still others, they are trying to establish facilities close to centers of expertise so they can gain access to more talent. As Asaf Farashuddin, the vice president of corporate strategy at the automobile components manufacturer Visteon, told the Booz researchers, "There's a lot of automotive intellect that's being generated now in the emerging markets, and you have to be in these markets to stay on the top of your game. And five years from now, you'll see some leading technology being developed first in India or China, and flowing back to the West."

A similar pressure toward relevant scale is being felt today in the U.S. health insurance industry, a sector with many small players. In the United States and elsewhere, for instance, there is a move toward digitized medical records, real-time adjudication of claims, and other information-based client services ("informatics"). But the new digital technologies and IT systems that enable these advances are not cheap, and they are beyond the reach of many smaller players. A corporate leader in this field might reasonably ask him- or herself, "How big must we get to afford these technologies?"

As companies consider this question, they also face a "make or buy" decision—whether to create the required innovation or operations improvement in-house or simply purchase it. What they often discover is that buying it via M&A has some innate financial advantages. If the investment can rapidly generate returns across the larger postintegration enterprise, instead of only across the original company, it makes the prospect of acquisition more attractive.

DEVELOPING RELEVANT SCALE: REACH AND DEPTH

To compete effectively, companies must gain the relevant scale they need in order to manage differences across marketplaces, deploy financial muscle, and increase customer wallet share. Astute leaders respond to these pressures by acquiring more relevant scale in two ways: reach and depth.

Reach

Reach is extending a company's customer base by expanding its presence into new markets or geographies while leveraging existing capabilities against those new opportunities. Often, this involves buying companies with complementary supply chains and customers. Expanding reach means securing a better market position, which often involves big, visible deals with recognizable name-brand companies.

When large banks buy up smaller banks and rebrand the acquired bank's branches in order to enlarge their deposit base or extend their territories, they are executing a reach strategy. Or consider the New York Stock Exchange's acquisition of the Euronext exchange in 2007. Euronext itself had been formed by the 2000 merger of the Amsterdam

Stock Exchange, the Brussels Stock Exchange, and the Paris Bourse—a deal conceived to take advantage of the harmonization of the European Union (EU) financial markets. After that, Euronext added the London International Financial Futures and Options Exchange (LIFFE) and the Portuguese stock exchange Bolsa de Valores de Lisboa e Porto (BVLP). The acquisitions that Euronext undertook and its eventual acquisition by the NYSE are all examples of extending reach.

Depth

Depth is acquiring new capabilities and assets to expand the company's business within the current customer base. This involves buying companies that can give the acquirer additional capacity and capabilities, or that bring related new product development opportunities. Companies can gain depth from an acquisition when they add a new technological prowess, a managerial skill, or a related product line to their corporate portfolios. In April 2008, the chocolate giant Mars Inc. bought the Wm. Wrigley Jr. chewing gum company, a deal so attractive that investing sage Warren Buffett committed $4.4 billion of the $23 billion all-cash offer. Mars left Wrigley as a stand-alone business after the deal, intending to make greater use of the capabilities that Wrigley could provide in launching and marketing confectionary products other than chocolate. Mars CEO Paul Michaels underlined this motive when he said that the deal was "not about being bigger—it's about being the best."

Both reach and depth are valuable, and some deals provide both. For example, Procter & Gamble's purchase

> **EXHIBIT 2-4 GILLETTE CEO JIM KILTS AND P&G CEO A. G. LAFLEY AS P&G BOUGHT GILLETTE**

Source: Shannon Stapleton/Reuters

of Gillette brought both new capabilities and expanded its depth and reach in global markets, in ways that specifically complemented P&G's other business units.

In addition to becoming the world's largest consumer products company, P&G moved more heavily into men's personal care products when, as seen in Exhibit 2-4, it closed the deal to acquire Gillette for $57 billion in 2005. [The photo shows P&G CEO A.G. Lafley (right) and Gillette CEO Jim Kilts addressing the New York Stock Exchange on the closing date, October 3; the backdrop was designed to show how Gillette's brands and technologies would fit with those of the acquiring company in complementary ways.] P&G realized that it could apply its world-class innovation, manufacturing, and marketing capabilities to Gillette's products and also push those products through a stronger and even more global distribution network. Meanwhile, Gillette's people had honed their own capabilities in product design and customer awareness. In their book *The Game-Changer*, P&G CEO A.G. Lafley and management expert Ram Charan credit the razor blade manufacturer with a rare ability for customer immersion: interpreting the contradictory responses from focus groups, for example, in ways that supported breakthrough innovation. This may seem like a small asset, but it made all the difference to the introduction of Gillette's bestselling Mach III razor, which consumers both loved and mocked when it was first prototyped in the late 1990s. Had they given more weight to the mockery, Gillette's innovators could easily have killed the product.

Similarly, when Johnson & Johnson bought Pfizer Consumer Healthcare, which included many powerful brands, such as Listerine, Sudafed, Rogaine, Nicorette, and Benadryl, in 2008, it made a very powerful combined reach and depth play. The acquisition brought J&J leading brands in nine additional product categories, including large new segments such as smoking cessation and mouthwash. J&J also gained capabilities in health-based marketing. Pfizer had learned to use its skills in consumer insight and clinical testing to create scientifically backed claims for its products—for example, that Listerine, when added to brushing and flossing, reduced plaque. J&J paid $16.6 billion (more than 20 times earnings) for the Pfizer division, which it quickly folded into its own consumer health-care products division, creating a $13 billion company, the "world's premier consumer health-care company," according to William Weldon, J&J's chairman and chief executive officer.

Not every deal can lead to increased reach *and* depth, but companies' efforts to achieve both through M&A are sure to continue. Neither organic growth nor alliances can build scale as quickly as M&A, and corporate leaders will need to build scale quickly to satisfy both their profit needs and their impatient investors.

PAST AND FUTURE

The ability of M&A to create relevant scale through the expansion of reach and depth depends upon a company's level of coherence after the deal is completed. This insight might seem obvious, but it represents a critical evolution beyond the prevailing conglomerate mindset that has held sway during the past 40 years.

In the 1970s and 1980s, many major companies adopted the conglomerate model, attempting to build coherence mainly through financial portfolio scale (for example, by acquiring countercyclical companies to smooth earnings). In some cases, deals were based on an overly optimistic view of the value of reach and depth. Travel conglomerates comprising airlines, hotels, and car rental agencies were set up. But these attempts were high-level agglomerations rather than truly integrated solutions to real customer problems.

Consumer products companies also underwent an era of large-scale consolidation. The transactions of the day were groundbreaking: Nabisco merged with Standard Brands in 1981; Philip Morris (now Altria) bought General Foods in 1985 and then acquired Kraft just three years later. Many of these mergers resulted in companies that were, in effect, portfolios of loosely related businesses. They often had different competitors and consumer bases, unrelated customer preferences, and different capabilities and drivers of success.

The spin-off of Conoco by DuPont in 1998, after nearly two decades, demonstrates that unlocking the full value of such acquisitions is difficult. DuPont bought Conoco in 1981 for $7.4 billion, the biggest deal in corporate history at that time, as a way to secure the petroleum feedstocks it needed to manufacture its products after the oil price crisis of 1979. But aside from vertical integration, the companies had little in common and were operated separately. During the following decade, as the price of oil dropped and DuPont shifted its strategic focus from petrochemicals to biotechnology, Conoco's value as a source of supply diminished. In 1999, a year after spinning off 20 percent of Conoco, DuPont sold its remaining shares to raise investment capital for other businesses.

In short, a more refined and nuanced view of attaining relevant scale through M&A has emerged in recent years. In place of the idea of multiple businesses under one roof, corporate leaders recognize that they can build a coherent growth strategy only by assembling a portfolio of coordinated assets and capabilities.

As they pursue this kind of growth, today's companies create relevant scale by many means other than sheer size. They leverage a variety of channels to market, such as the Internet, and they exploit new technologies, such as nanotechnology, across multiple business lines. And they increasingly apply the test of coherence to their corporate development activities, making deals that complement and build upon their core capabilities *and* divesting those units that dilute coherence. This process is clearly on display when a company slims down in one area through divestitures and bulks up in another through M&A.

For instance, in recent years, the H.J. Heinz Company has sold off over $3 billion in noncore businesses, such as seafood and poultry. It used the proceeds from these divestitures to grow its three core businesses (its iconic ketchup, condiments, and sauces business; its line of meals and snacks; and its infant nutrition group) and to bolster them with acquisitions, such as its $855 million deal to buy HP Foods from the French food group Danone in 2005. With HP Foods came the HP and Lea & Perrins sauce brands, which are especially popular in Europe, and this acquisition helped the company deliver record sales of $4 billion in its ketchup, condiments, and sauces business in fiscal 2008.

The Linde Group, an international industrial gases and engineering company based in Germany, represents an example of coherence in industrial products. Linde underwent a major transformation in September 2006 following the acquisition of its U.K.-based competitor The BOC Group. Linde's former materials-handling business was rebranded as KION Group and sold to KKR and Goldman Sachs in November 2006 for $5.1 billion. In March 2007, the BOC Edwards semiconductor equipment business was sold to CCMP Capital for $900 million. These divestitures recast the Linde Group as the world's largest pure-play industrial gases supplier, a far more focused and profitable worldwide entity.

As scale becomes more and more relevant, its benefits expand from traditional cost synergies to increased wallet share, investment leverage, more easily defended customer positions, and the enhanced ability to rapidly capture adjacent growth opportunities. Because of these benefits, the corporate drive for relevant scale—more specifically, for depth, reach, and enhanced coherence—is an enduring trend that affects not just mergers and acquisitions, but all forms of corporate growth. The future is shaping up to be a fluid, mix-and-match environment, and to survive, companies must put potential mergers and acquisitions—and divestitures—in the context of long-term growth development that intertwines these activities with organic growth and alliances.

Leadership must think in merganic terms. The leading companies of the next decade will be prepared—organizationally, structurally, and culturally—for flexible, multifaceted growth; they will constantly group and regroup their assets and capabilities, seeing what fits and what doesn't, filling in the gaps, and then jettisoning the peripheral, nonessential elements. And as we discuss further in Chapter 7, leaders will need a rigorous approach—a tightly linked, chained sequence of expansions that meet the coherence test at each stage and ensure that their growth plans will yield relevant scale and its benefits. They will thus gain new insight into what capabilities they need, which they should buy, how they should buy them, when they should buy them, and the order in which they should buy them. And this will also help prepare them for the next big trend facing them: the velocity of capital.

3

VELOCITY AND IMPATIENCE

Once upon a time, a mere 20 years ago, if you wanted to buy 100 shares of General Electric stock, you would telephone your stockbroker to place the order. The broker, in turn, would phone an order taker on the floor of the exchange, who wrote the order and handed it to a runner. The runner raced across the crowded din of the exchange to find the pit trader—the person who actually conducted the transaction. The pit trader read the order, listened to any other instructions from the runner, and then shouted across a sea of hands and heads to find a seller of those 100 shares of GE. If a seller was found, the trade was made and the runner returned to the order taker, confirming that your order had been filled. If the pit trader couldn't find a seller, your order was handed off to a specialist—a broker's broker on the exchange floor—who kept a list of unfilled orders and looked for opportunities to execute the order throughout the day.

EXHIBIT 3-1 A TRADER AT THE NYSE, APRIL 2008

Source: Seth Wenig/AP Photo

Today, to buy those 100 shares of GE stock, you click a mouse and somewhere a microprocessor in a black box on a metal shelf in a windowless room silently matches the trade in a fraction of a second. Another fraction of a second later, other investors know that the transaction has occurred. These little black boxes work so well that by the end of 2007, NYSE Euronext had closed three of its five trading rooms in New York City. When you visit an exchange today, you see a very different scene; Exhibit 3-1 shows a trader on the floor at the New York Stock Exchange just before the markets opened on April 24, 2008. There are far more computers than people involved.

What's most remarkable about this evolution—even more remarkable than the speed with which it has occurred, the huge costs it has wrung from the process, and the impact it has had on business culture—is the way it is taken for granted. It's easy to forget that as recently as the early 1990s, when the world was adjusting to a post-Soviet landscape and the reunification of Germany, floor runners were central to virtually every trade—just as they had been for generations. No more. (And while the full impact of the 2008 market meltdown is uncertain, it's clear that decentralization and digital technology in financial markets added to the breadth of the crisis and the speed with which it spread.)

Technology—specifically, the power of the computer and the reach of the Internet—has bestowed unprecedented reach, leverage, and velocity on every aspect of business today. Cottage industries with global reach have sprung up around services such as eBay, enabled by technology to trade in the most eclectic of goods and services with the utmost ease. The market for credit default swaps, which were virtually nonexistent in 2000 and were impossible without recent advances in technology, ballooned to more than $40 trillion in 2007 and (by some estimates) as much as $60 trillion in 2008.

Technology has also enabled investors of all sorts—from Middle East sovereign wealth fund managers to midwestern soccer moms in the United States—to participate in financial markets. And it's not just financial markets that have sped up: "just-in-time" inventory strategies, real-time monitoring at points of sale, instantaneous credit approvals, and online sales have stepped up the velocity of business in general. Energy (particularly in the form of electricity), services, and even physical goods are moving further, faster, and more efficiently than they ever have before. Knowledge workers remain plugged into their jobs 24/7 via their BlackBerries, even on "getaway" vacations. Copies of the dresses that movie stars wear to the Oscar awards ceremony appear in discount stores within a few days; quick-serve restaurants measure the time it takes to serve hungry customers in seconds. Even innovations where long lead times were expected—new pharmaceuticals, advances in polymers, and creative architectural designs—now face nearly immediate competition from fast followers and look-alikes.

Many aspects of the business world seem poised to change, particularly in response to the credit crisis of 2008 and the global recession, but no one is arguing that either stock exchanges or supply chains should go back to their slower and more insular forms. Velocity is here to stay, and it will only increase during the years to come.

This is not just a technological shift; it represents a sea change in the culture of business. Accelerated connection and competition are compelling financial players and business managers alike to press hard for even tiny improvements and to move quickly to avoid missteps and losses. When one company adopts an innovation, if it isn't unique to that company's culture and capabilities, then others will rapidly follow suit.

Hence the title of William Barnett's book about this phenomenon, *The Red Queen Syndrome among Organizations*. Like the character in Lewis Carroll's classic children's story *Through the Looking Glass*, it really does take "all the running you can do, to keep in the same place." The Red Queen Syndrome breeds urgency in decision making and an intense impatience for results. The old maxim that time is money was never more finely sliced or more fervently embraced.

The impact of high business velocity on the practice of mergers and acquisitions is immense and fundamental. This impact in itself is not necessarily dangerous—until the ingredient of impatience is added.

A CULTURE OF IMPATIENCE

Traders have always been known for brash impatience and competitiveness; it seems to go with the profession. But those qualities were always mitigated by built-in limits: some related to the geographical isolation of distant markets from one another, and some related to the traditional 9-to-5 boundaries of the business day. All these limits have eroded during the past 20 years. No matter how much regulators restrict specific practices, there is no way to legally mandate better judgment or thoughtful decision making by forcing people to slow down their trades. The instantaneous connectivity and cultural impatience that was once unique to the trading world has now become the norm in all aspects of business.

The interconnectedness of physical and financial markets—which was brought about by technology and the participation of more economies in the world's capital markets—means that investments can be made in more directions, more easily, than ever before. This liquidity has been a boon for those who are selling goods and raising capital (as long as they can make their offerings attractive). It is also a boon for buyers and investors who are looking for the best product, because it enables them to move rapidly and across great distances. But for those who are seeking patience and perspective, interconnectedness creates a constant set of pressures and distractions that are hard to overcome.

Consider the rise of after-hours call centers. Customers now routinely place orders or ask questions from halfway around the world; serving them requires 24/7 transaction capabilities, meaning that there's little built-in rest or downtime for a supplier any more. The customers who dial into these call centers expect to get an immediate high-quality response. The products that are sold and serviced through these call centers must be conceived, designed, and brought to market faster than ever because increased velocity and reduced product differentiation have conferred ever greater advantages on first movers. As businesses become more capable in meeting these challenges, the resulting compressed competition has dramatically narrowed the differences among products, services, and suppliers. Business has become like professional golf; competitors are so talented that the outcome of a long tournament often boils down to a single bounce or some fortuitous timing.

Intertwined with 24-hour, lightning-fast operational and transactional demands is round-the-clock, real-time information. Militants in the Niger River Delta kidnap foreign oil workers; a tropical depression forms in the mid-Atlantic; the United States agrees to provide nuclear power assistance to India; a new clothing line suddenly becomes fashionable; Jamaica sweeps the women's 100 meters in Beijing; a government passes a measure to invest billions in an industry; and within minutes, the news about this, and relevant commentary, is available to millions of people. Whether they're about weather, politics, sports, or economics, today's news headlines and news minutiae are blasted around the globe in a relentless 24-hour cycle. BlackBerries, the Internet, and cable never sleep. Near-instantaneous information and near-infinite reach have been married with near-simultaneous movement. Both investors and customers are more aware of each other than ever before; when a fad strikes, both can change direction on a dime, often joining the herd when they see which way their peers are moving.

Competition for investments is another driver of velocity and impatience. Even after the meltdown, there is a huge amount of wealth seeking returns in the world today compared to the relatively finite number of places that the money can go, especially given the diminished trust that many investors feel after the losses they have endured. The result is intense competition for the best and safest uses of capital. This increase in demand raises the cost of the most attractive investments and makes it more difficult to produce superior results.

Naturally, this increase in velocity makes many investors edgy and impatient. Intensely aware of the opportunity cost of keeping their money in an underperforming investment, they're willing to act quickly as opportunities arise. In the aftermath of the meltdown, the nature of the available opportunities may change, but the pressure to take advantage of them—more rapidly than anyone else does—will, if anything, be greater than it was before.

Velocity and impatience have fundamentally changed business management practice. Thoughtful long-term plans gave way to annual cycles, which were dominated by quarterly reporting; then newer technologies enabled daily reporting on metrics such as revenue by location and customer order fulfillment. Small differences have become amplified. Small stumbles become evident more quickly and broadly now, sometimes with career consequences. Reports of more than ten pages or three bullets on a page are ignored. The reflective retreat has given way to a fast-paced videoconference (with half the attendees multitasking), and an invitation to a prestigious conference is often met with a "Who has time for that?" response.

Equally telling is the influence of velocity and impatience on employees. Twenty years ago, résumés were much shorter. But since then, the social contract between employee and employer has been rewritten. The decline of defined-benefit pension plans and the frequency of layoffs have created a workforce that is more conditioned to switching to new employers for new challenges and better pay. Most employers, for their part, are no longer leery of long résumés. For future generations, the pace will probably increase. Business managers and consumers from the "millennial generation"—those born between 1978 and 2000—are already known to be impatient and demanding about their career progression and services.

For all of these reasons, today's production, consumer, financial, and talent markets are frenetic. Because people can transact business all day and all night long, they must and they do. Once, executives could literally sleep on it when contemplating a decision. Now, fewer and fewer customers and investors are willing to wait a day for an answer. Years ago, the senior leader of a major company was heard to say, "Any five-minute stretch without making a decision is a waste of time." That seemed outlandish back then; now, it's just business as usual.

THE DEMANDS ON M&A LEADERSHIP

The impact of velocity and impatience makes M&A and other forms of deal making trickier than ever. Leaders

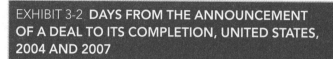

EXHIBIT 3-2 **DAYS FROM THE ANNOUNCEMENT OF A DEAL TO ITS COMPLETION, UNITED STATES, 2004 AND 2007**

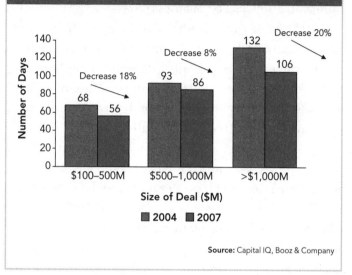

Source: Capital IQ, Booz & Company

who hope to satisfy investors' demands for returns, meet customers' desire for new products and services, create career opportunities to attract and retain bright employees, and remain an attractive business partner have less time to achieve ever more aggressive growth levels. And they are hard-pressed to build such growth through purely organic means. The pressures of velocity and impatience push managers not only to act but to act quickly.

The resulting effect on mergers can be seen in Exhibit 3-2. It shows how the speed with which deals are consummated has increased between 2004 and 2007. In the United States, the average time to completion for deals of all sizes has decreased; for mega-deals, the time has been reduced by 20 percent. The distress sales in the U.S. financial sector in 2008 have reduced these times even more. Wells Fargo, for instance, announced its $15.1 billion deal for Wachovia on October 3, 2008 and closed on January 1, 2009, just 62 business days later.

At the same time, this haste is taking a toll on the effectiveness of deals. Mergers and acquisitions are complex transactions at the best of times; they inevitably have their setbacks, missteps, and frustrations. Moreover, M&A stumbles, or even perceived stumbles, can provoke legal or financial penalties that are both harsh and swift. Yet with the increasingly impatient and activist dispositions of investors, customers, employees, and business partners, there is less and less tolerance for delays and errors.

Once a deal is announced, a "get on with it" mentality often takes hold among many stakeholders. You can clearly hear that in the language that is being used about deals, such as "Be ready to implement on Day One," "quick wins," and "30-day plans." This impatience compresses the time available for thoughtful planning. Anyone who suggests a more measured approach, or who expresses concern about the risks of haste, is deemed to "not get it." Even when a careful plan for postclose integration and follow-up has been laid out, it's difficult to find the time and patience needed to attend to the details.

In short, managers face a conundrum. Integration planning and execution of mergers and acquisitions takes time, and time should be allotted for them. Yet deal makers operate in a world where financial and market expectations won't allow them much time.

This combination of a stepped-up pace and increased risk represents a major challenge for the executives overseeing deals, and it also extends to other key players whose cooperation can be critical to M&A success. Defections among impatient key stakeholders—executives, board members, large investors, regulators, unions, and employees—can trigger sell-offs, devaluation, customer attrition, and a weakened competitive position. If regulators see that the markets are reacting negatively to a deal, they may be more willing to impose restrictions on or reject deals that require their approval. Union leaders may feel that they have more leverage to negotiate better terms. And "brain drain" is an ever-present threat; employees on both sides of a deal are more willing to jump ship if they perceive that their futures might be negatively affected.

How do successful leaders respond to these conditions during a merger or acquisition? Speed at any cost is not the best answer.

First, executives must be trained and be prepared to move with the greatest haste, yet still act with thoughtful deliberation. The best analogy is to an experienced emergency room or airline crew, who are practiced and drilled to the point where diagnoses occur quickly and action can be taken with speed and confidence. These actions are guided by predetermined protocols, but they are informed by the situational judgments of the professionals on the scene—in effect, a rapid response team trained and put in place before the deals begin.

Second, M&A leaders in today's world need predetermined game plans and a comprehensive merganic road map to guide their actions. The best M&A practitioners create interlocking plans, covering immediate, medium-term, and long-term time frames, that integrate the short-term exigencies with the deal's desired end states.

➤ *1,000-day plan:* A well-conceived integration plan articulates an end state (perhaps at 1,000 days, but often sooner for some activities and longer for others). This design fits the business rationale for the deal and demonstrates how the resulting firm can sustain a long-term positive outcome. This might include paying back any debt incurred in the transaction, reinforcing and, if necessary, realizing the new strategic direction that dictated the deal in the first place, and laying the foundation for the next stages of organic growth and capability development.

➤ *100-day plan:* Few investors (and few executives) are interested in waiting three years to see results. Thus, during the merger planning phase, corporate leaders typically create a medium-term implementation plan, including revenue expansion, cost reductions, and the combining of operations. The definition of "medium term" varies, but it is usually long enough to substantiate the logic of the deal and to demonstrate that the company is capable of executing the integration plan.

➤ *Immediate plan:* Often referred to as the "Day One plan," this describes not only what will happen on the first day but how the combined entity will manage during the time between the close and the beginning of integration. How, for example, will the newly combined managers make the decisions required in the first week or month after the close? In addition, this plan provides those investors, customers, and other constituents who are focused on the immediate benefits of the deal with tangible evidence of progress.

An integration approach that is solely oriented toward the long term will not appease today's high-velocity, impatient stakeholders. But the often-seen tendency to focus only on the short term, and to defer longer-term planning until later, is like attempting to steer a speeding car by looking only at the pavement five feet ahead of the bumper. Deal makers must simultaneously link the need for immediate signs of progress with the need to stay on track toward the long-term goals. The job of ensuring that these time horizons are part of one integrated plan falls into the hands of the integration leadership designated by both companies.

The trick, of course, is to ensure leadership excellence throughout the M&A process. The chief executive of the newly combined company, in particular, sets the tone for the entire M&A transaction, from planning to deal making to execution. This individual must translate the strategic logic behind the deal and establish realistic expectations for all the constituents involved: shareholders, employees, partners, and the financial markets at large. If the CEO fails to do this, he or she risks the flight of capital, people, and, most likely, the CEO's own support bases. And that, in turn, exacerbates the impatience and places greater pressure on the entire company.

IMPATIENCE AND THE CEO

The need for growth through organic expansion, mergers and acquisitions, and partnerships helps explain why performance pressure on today's corporate leaders, particularly CEOs, is greater than it has ever been before.

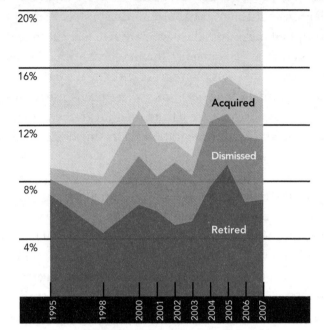

Source: Booz & Company; "The Performance Paradox," by Per-Ola Karlsson, Gary L. Neilson, and Juan Carlos Webster, *strategy+business*, Summer 2008

Probably the most visible evidence of this pressure is the wave of "forced succession" in the C-suite. An ongoing Booz & Company study found that annual rates of turnover of CEOs in the top 2,500 publicly held companies worldwide increased by *54 percent* between 1995 and 2007. In that period, shown as "Dismissed" in Exhibit 3-3, performance-related turnover—cases in which CEOs were fired or otherwise forced to leave—increased from about

1 percent to about 4 percent of these companies, a four-fold jump. The growing role that mergers and acquisitions play in CEO turnover is also evident in this chart: while CEO retirements and dismissals (for non-M&A-related reasons) have both declined since 2005, the number of CEOs who lost their jobs because of a merger or acquisition has been steadily rising for the past five years, increasing almost as much as the forced dismissals.

To be sure, the pressure on CEOs is as much a matter of perception as it is of reality. Close examination of the data reveals a remarkable fact: both in 1995 and in 2007, CEOs who delivered substandard returns to investors were just as likely to achieve long tenure as CEOs who delivered above-average returns. On the other hand, there are some signs of a trend toward greater financial accountability. We see this trend, for example, when poor performance is extreme: CEOs around the world whose companies performed in the bottom 10 percent of the 2,500 public companies in 2007 were almost four times as likely to be dismissed as CEOs whose companies were in the top 10 percent. The perception that CEOs have their necks on the line may not be backed up entirely by the data, but it is grounded enough in reality to drive behavior, particularly in pushing companies toward measures like M&A that lead to faster growth.

THE JOY OF BEING A TARGET

In some cases, particularly after a turnaround, the best possible thing that could happen (for shareholders, at least, and maybe for employees as well)

EXHIBIT 3-4 MERGER CEOS DELIVER BETTER STOCK PERFORMANCE

ANNUAL RETURN TO INVESTORS RELATIVE TO A BROAD MARKET AVERAGE

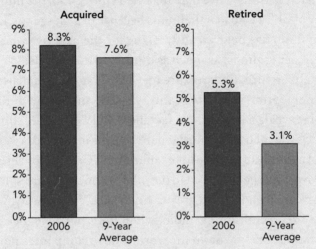

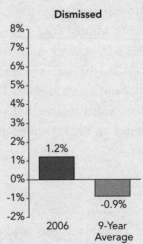

Source: Booz & Company; "The Era of the Inclusive Leader," by Chuck Lucier, Steven Wheeler, and Rolf Habbel, *strategy+business*, Summer 2007

is to be acquired by another company. That's the implication of a study conducted by Booz & Company in 2007 on CEO succession rates and their relationship to mergers and acquisitions.

Over the course of nine years, from 1995 to 2006, CEOs who lost their jobs when their companies were acquired or taken private generated returns to investors that were, on average, greater than those of CEOs who reached their planned retirement age or were dismissed for poor performance. In fact, as shown in Exhibit 3-4, the stocks of companies whose CEOs left because of an acquisition had an annual return of 7.6 percent over the course of the previous nine years—more than twice as much as companies whose CEOs simply retired.

To be sure, these CEOs generated above-average returns in part because of the acquisition premium when the company was sold. But the data show that there is more to the story; companies tend to become acquisition targets after several years of good performance. This phenomenon (which was observed in a sample of 2,500 publicly traded companies around the world) might be labeled the "merger multiplier."

This is not to say that investors ought to demand that companies try to be acquired, or that any acquisition offer represents a premium to the current valuation. Some CEOs, such as Fujio Cho and Tatsuro Toyoda at Toyota and Bill Gates at Microsoft, create great returns for investors by keeping their companies independent and building them into much larger and more valuable businesses. But for nearly one-third of the chief executives, selling the company is an element of a strategy to create outsized returns. Thus, boards and CEOs should strongly consider the possibility that being acquired offers the best strategic opportunity for the company and creates the best returns to investors.

Profiting through being an acquisition target is an especially attractive strategy for an "outsider CEO"—someone who is brought in by the board from an external position and charged with turning around a poorly performing company. When the work of exiting underperforming businesses, significantly reducing costs, and forcing change in a corporation's culture is complete, performance tends to drop off. Selling the company once the turnaround is successful takes full advantage of a CEO's up-front restructuring skills and increases the value of acquisition offers without requiring the external CEO to be equally effective in driving long-term growth.

SMART IS BEAUTIFUL

Merganic strategy and the right kind of execution, which are described in greater detail in Chapters 7 and 8, can help chief executives cope with the velocity and impatience that surrounds M&A. A merganic road map positions individual deals in the overall context of the company's future and helps companies avoid a transactional mindset that limits strategic thinking. Further, CEOs who can articulate this more comprehensive, coherent strategy to investors and other stakeholders—and, of course, who can live up to its milestones—can better manage those stakeholders' pervasive impatience. In fact, the CEOs can even earn the ultimate luxury of additional time to produce results because stakeholders tend to be more patient when they know where management is headed and see evidence of a sound and coherent strategic vision.

For instance, one CEO of an Australia-based building products company began laying the groundwork for a merger long before he had even identified a merger partner. As he pursued discussions with potential targets, he simultaneously educated his board and his shareholders on the forces pushing the company to seek a merger. He characterized this effort as "earning the right to do a deal." When he finally announced a target, the support he needed was already in place and committed.

Johnson & Johnson is another company that appears to have won the support of investors in its M&A initiatives. The company pursues waves of related acquisitions in a variety of businesses—consumer products, pharmaceuticals, devices and diagnostics, drug delivery, and biotech—aimed at building specific capabilities that reinforce one another and provide relevant scale. The ability of senior executives to communicate these themes to investors, and to show how the acquisitions will deliver value, buys J&J time to produce results and engenders patience during the company's occasional setbacks.

Conversely, even good deals can suffer when impatience takes hold. One such case was the merger of Glaxo Wellcome and SmithKline Beecham in 2000 to form what was then the world's largest pharmaceutical company. The merger was positioned as an innovation-based deal—the companies needed to combine their money to invest in new drug research.

Recalls former SmithKline Beecham CFO Andrew Bonfield, for whom this was the largest merger of his career: "The shareholders who supported the deal have been saying ever since, 'Where's the pipeline [of new drugs]?' The pity is that, financially, this deal was impeccably executed. The returns have been unbelievable. If the merged company had been sold as a purely financial deal, the company probably could have done another."

In the end, when it comes to executing deals effectively, the most successful companies will not be the ones that conduct the most deals, the biggest deals, or even the fastest deals. The most successful companies will be those that can move with deliberate speed. Like a pilot facing engine failure or an emergency room doctor, these corporate leaders will be prepared to respond rapidly in a holistic manner and will cultivate the dedicated skills and processes needed to execute deals quickly and judiciously.

The mid-twentieth-century economist Leopold Kohr once argued that "slow is beautiful"—that the problems raised by human society were dramatically increased when the pace of activity sped up. Kohr was wrong; a focus on slowness tends to lead to lethargy and complacency. But as William Barnett's Red Queen tells us, speeding up activity is not, in itself, sufficient to cope with velocity and impatience. In the years to come, there will be an increasing premium placed on strategic savvy, deal capability, and experience. Smart is beautiful.

4

THE RISE OF
NEW BLUES

IN THE 1990s, there were no large private companies in China, and certainly no Chinese firms were among the world's 25 largest companies. But by September 2007, China was home to three of the world's largest companies by market capitalization. One of them, the Industrial and Commercial Bank of China, had recently overtaken Citigroup as the world's largest bank.

China is not the only country that is building an impressive corporate power base. In 1990, there were only 19 companies from developing economies listed in the Fortune Global 500; in 2008, the number had risen to 74, as seen in Exhibit 4-1. In broader terms, from the early 1990s to the mid-2000s, the total number of multinational companies whose parents were based in Brazil, China, India, and the Republic of Korea grew 450 percent, from less than 2,700 companies to more than 14,800. The Middle East and South Africa have also launched companies with

EXHIBIT 4-1 NEW BLUES IN THE 2008 FORTUNE GLOBAL 500 BY NATIONAL HEADQUARTERS

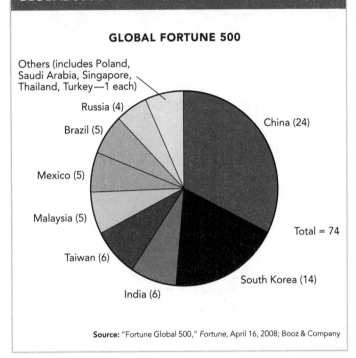

GLOBAL FORTUNE 500

Others (includes Poland, Saudi Arabia, Singapore, Thailand, Turkey—1 each)

Russia (4)

Brazil (5)

Mexico (5)

Malaysia (5)

Taiwan (6)

India (6)

China (24)

Total = 74

South Korea (14)

Source: "Fortune Global 500," *Fortune*, April 16, 2008; Booz & Company

global aspirations; for example, Saudi Basic Industries Corporation (SABIC) purchased General Electric Company's plastics unit in May 2007, thus becoming one of the world's largest producers of high-performance polymers. SABMiller, formerly South African Breweries, is now the world's second-largest beer maker.

These are indicators of a radical and ongoing reordering of the leading companies in the global capital markets. A new class of blue chip company is emerging: the *New Blues* are corporate bellwethers from emerging markets that can compete toe-to-toe with the largest and most powerful companies in the West for acquisition and alliance partners. The New Blues include companies such as Haier and Lenovo in China, the Tata Group in India, Arcelik in Turkey, Ingenuity Solutions in Malaysia, Bionova in Mexico, and Cordlife in Singapore.

Steven Wallace, Citigroup's head of M&A for the Asia-Pacific region, might have been speaking about companies based in emerging countries around the world when he said, "Asian companies are taking advantage of strong balance sheets and ready access to capital to create regional champions capable of becoming major global players, in sectors ranging from industrials to resources."

The New Blues are succeeding for many reasons, but thriving home economies with burgeoning middle classes are particularly notable factors in their growth. Indeed, their achievements are helping to create and reinforce these conditions, and are breeding greater ambition. Some of these companies started as low-cost contract manufacturers or outsourcers, but they have progressed far beyond that role. They are creating branded products for their home markets and for developed nations as well.

The New Blues are very strong competitors. Their cost base and relatively new, often more efficient operations give them an advantage in mature markets. They also enjoy inherent advantages over their Western competitors in emerging markets outside their home countries. They have a natural and well-honed expertise for operating in developing markets, and since they are growing up alongside the middle classes in these markets, they have an innate understanding of this new economic group's needs and desires. Often their products and services are a natural fit for nearby emerging markets, and this also puts them in an excellent position to thrive and make acquisitions in their own backyards.

THE NEW BLUES STEP OUT

The aspirational drive of the New Blues to create businesses with top-notch capabilities, market positions, and brands is having a fundamental effect on the global M&A arena. Evidence for this assertion can be seen in the growing percentage of outbound cross-border M&A stemming from companies in developing nations, as shown in Exhibit 4-2. It can also be seen in the continuing activity and the near-term intentions of the New Blues themselves.

The merger and acquisition activity of the New Blues has been particularly noteworthy since 2005. In some respects, it has reached a tipping point, rivaling and surpassing the M&A levels of Western companies.

In China, for instance, investment in foreign enterprise grew 25.6 percent to $95.8 billion between 2000 and 2007, according to a Leeds University Business School study published in *China Review*. The latter year was a pivotal year in terms of corporate investments. That was the first year in which Chinese companies spent more money on cross-border deals (about $24.2 billion) than foreign companies spent acquiring companies in China (about $22 billion), according to Thomson Financial. In 2008, China's cross-border M&A fell by 30 percent compared to 2007, but remained active, according to market research firm Zero2IPO Group. Meanwhile, China's state-owned enterprises are calling for the government to ease restrictions on offshore acquisitions; among other reasons, they

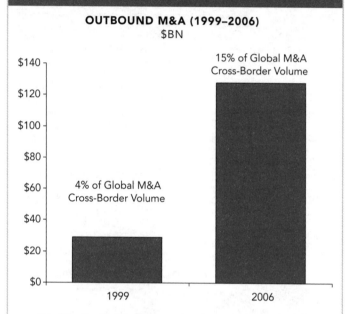

EXHIBIT 4-2 VOLUME OF NEW BLUES'S OUTBOUND CROSS-BORDER M&A, 1999 AND 2006 (IN BILLIONS OF DOLLARS)

OUTBOUND M&A (1999–2006)
$BN

15% of Global M&A Cross-Border Volume

4% of Global M&A Cross-Border Volume

Note: "New Blues" includes M&A transactions of companies from developing countries, including CIS and southeastern Europe. "Outbound" is defined as M&A transactions where the target is headquartered outside the region of the headquarters of the acquiring company.

Source: U.N. Conference on Trade and Development

want to take advantage of the plummeting valuations among foreign companies in the oil and mining industries to help attain price stability in their sourcing of raw materials.

Outbound deal volume is growing in India, too. In 2007, Tata Steel's $14.8 billion merger with Anglo-Dutch steelmaker Corus created the fifth-largest company in the global steel industry. The wide-ranging list of Indian deals also includes Hindalco's $6 billion acquisition of Canadian

EXHIBIT 4-3 TOP 10 ACQUISITIONS BY INDIAN AND CHINESE COMPANIES ANNOUNCED IN 2006–2007

INDIA TOP 10—ANNOUNCED IN 2006–2007

Date Closed	Target	$M	Buyer	Target HQ
04/02/2007	Corus Group Limited	14,853	Tata Steel Limited	United Kingdom
05/15/2007	Novelis Inc.	6,033	Hindalco Industries Ltd.	Canada
06/20/2007	Algoma Steel Inc.	1,570	Essar Steel Ltd.	United States
05/16/2007	Whyte & Mackay Ltd.	1,180	United Spirits Ltd.	United Kingdom
09/21/2006	Omimex De Columbia Ltd.	850	Natural Gas Corporation Videsh Ltd.	Colombia
09/29/2007	Jindal United Steel Corporation/Saw Pipes USA, Ir	810	JSW Steel Ltd.	United States
08/25/2006	Energy Brands Inc.	677	Tata Sons Limited, Tata Tea (GB) Ltd.	United States
07/19/2007	Rain CII Carbon, LLC	595	Rain Calcining Ltd.	United States
01/31/2006	Al Furat Petroleum Company	581	Oil and Natural Gas Corp. Ltd.	Syria
03/03/2006	Betapharm Arzneimittel GmbH	572	Dr. Reddy's Laboratories Ltd.	Germany

CHINA TOP 10—ANNOUNCED IN 2006–2007

Date Closed	Target	$M	Buyer	Target HQ
02/14/2008	Standard Bank Group Ltd.	5,600	Industrial and Commercial Bank of China	South Africa
08/10/2006	JSC Udmurtneft-Burenie	3,630	China Petroleum & Chemical Corp.	Russia
12/28/2006	PetroKazakhstan Inc.	2,735	PetroChina Col. Ltd.	Canada
04/19/2006	South Atlantic Petroleum Ltd., OML 130	2,692	CNOOC Ltd.	Nigeria
12/19/2006	Tubatse Chrome Corporation	2,000	Sinosteel Corporation	South Africa
01/01/2007	CITIC Canada Petroleum Limited	1,910	CITIC Group Company	Canada
12/12/2007	CITIC Canada Petroleum Limited	1,004	CITIC Resources Holdings Ltd.	Canada
06/27/2007	OJSC Karazhanbasmunai	1,004	CITIC Resources Holdings Ltd.	Kazakhstan
12/15/2006	BOC Aviation	965	Bank of China	Singapore
09/21/2006	Omimex De Colombia Ltd.	850	China Petroleum & Chemical Corp. Oil	Colombia

aluminum roller Novelis, Inc., and United Spirits' $1.2 billion acquisition of Whyte & Mackay, the U.K. distiller. Exhibit 4-3 shows the top 10 acquisitions announced by Indian and Chinese companies in 2006 and 2007.

All indications suggest, notwithstanding the downturn of 2008-2009, that the New Blues will continue to set their sights on the world's developed markets. In 2006 and 2007, for instance, Chinese companies directed 53 percent of their M&A transaction volume to companies in the United States and Canada. Companies in other Asian nations were the next most common targets of Chinese M&A, accounting for 26 percent of the volume, or just under half as much. In the personal computer industry, which was long controlled by U.S. firms, several Asian companies are now among the top five. In 2004, Lenovo, a Chinese firm, acquired IBM's PC division and is now the fourth-largest PC maker in the world. (Although its global business slipped at the end of 2008, leading to a highly publicized change in management, Lenovo continues to dominate the Chinese market, where the middle class and entrepreneurs are discovering PCs and driving a growth rate that is four times that in the U.S. market.) In 2007, Taiwanese PC maker Acer bought Gateway to gain entry into the U.S. market, becoming the third-largest PC manufacturer globally; then, in January 2008, it strengthened its competitive position in Europe by acquiring a 75 percent controlling interest in Packard Bell, a PC maker based in the Netherlands.

The New Blues will compete with increasing strength for U.S.- and Europe-based assets, through both M&A and direct financial investment. Chinese companies, for example, are building their experience with acquisitions around the world, often targeting advantaged assets, such as iconic brands and business-cycle-proof infrastructure. While Western companies try to pick acquisition targets and alliance partners in emerging markets, companies from emerging nations will quietly buy up undervalued or promising companies in the United States and Europe.

In the process of entering the industrialized world, however, the New Blues will run into (and will sometimes provoke) new roadblocks. For example, labor dynamics may hinder the expansion attempts of the New Blues in the United States and Europe. Already, American and European trade unions are pushing for succession clauses in their labor contracts; these clauses protect jobs in the event of an acquisition and hold great sway at the deal-making table. In 2006, the United Steelworkers Union scuttled the Brazilian steel giant CSN's attempt to buy Wheeling Pittsburgh Steel and paved the way for a successful bid by Chicago-based Esmark, which promised no layoffs. Another potential barrier to entry is the Sarbanes-Oxley Act in the United States, which has created demanding financial disclosure and accounting rules that New Blues—and even some multinationals from Europe—find burdensome. Europe, for its part, has stiff agricultural tariffs and rules about carbon trading that must be considered by any outside company seeking M&A opportunities.

Finally, the cumulative effect of the New Blues' success will trigger reactions. In March 2009, the Australian Foreign Investment Review Board expressed concern about Chinese investment in the Australian natural resources sector. This was triggered by several events: China Minmetal's $3.6 billion offer for OZ Minerals, Hunan Valin Iron & Steel's attempt to buy a minority stake in Fortescue

Metals, and Chinalco's $19.5 billion investment in the Rio Tinto mining giant. As part of the justification for the deal, Rio's management said there would be increased access to exploration ground in China. Even more telling was the rationale of added access to Chinese investors, such as the Export/Import Bank of China. This logic in itself was not new; but suddenly an emerging-market New Blue bank was proposed as the potential financier for an established global company, rather than the reverse.

In the end, the pressure for global M&A will probably outweigh the barriers and roadblocks. Too many companies are seeking to compete outside their home countries, and political leaders understand that a restrictive environment at home creates limits on their companies' opportunities abroad. Some commentators foresee a kind of "new mercantilism," in which particular countries—or regions—use trade barriers to create advantage for their own companies. That will inevitably happen to some extent, but it will always be tempered by the knowledge that if it becomes too prevalent or blatant, other countries will respond in kind.

THE BEER CASE: FROM LOCAL TALENT TO GLOBAL STAGE

The New Blues have not sprung up overnight. Instead, their emergence has been and continues to be an evolving process. In each stage of their growth, the number of potential New Blues gets winnowed down as competition becomes more intense and growing regional companies become acquisition targets themselves. This process is well illustrated by the consolidation in the Latin American beer industry over the last quarter century, from which only one brewer, AmBev of Brazil, emerged as a fully fledged New Blue.

In the 1980s and 1990s, leading brewers in Latin America recognized the strong correlation between profitability and market share and began consolidating their positions in their home markets through mergers and acquisitions. Once this initial wave of consolidation was complete, several brewers tried to maintain their growth through diversification within their countries: Mexico's Femsa expanded into beverages; Polar in Venezuela expanded into snacks, food, and beverages; and Columbia's Bavaria invested in everything from telecommunications to airlines. But these forays, which lacked coherence and relevant scale, generally proved disappointing.

At the same time, however, cross-border markets began to open to the brewers. Trade agreements such as Mercosur, the Andean Pact (now known as the Andean Community), and NAFTA paved the way for a new regional wave of consolidation, as shown in Exhibit 4-4. AmBev from Brazil acquired Quilmes in Argentina. Bavaria acquired the Panamanian brewery Cervecería Nacional and further consolidated its positions in Ecuador, Colombia, and Peru by purchasing CCN, Cervecería Leona, and Backus, respectively. (It gained control of Backus only after doing battle with Polar, which had a stake in the company.)

EXHIBIT 4-4 CONSOLIDATION IN THE LATIN AMERICAN BEER INDUSTRY

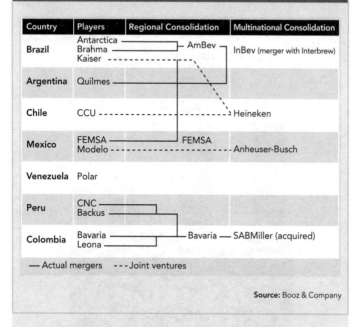

Country	Players	Regional Consolidation	Multinational Consolidation
Brazil	Antarctica Brahma Kaiser	AmBev	InBev (merger with Interbrew)
Argentina	Quilmes		
Chile	CCU		Heineken
Mexico	FEMSA Modelo	FEMSA	Anheuser-Busch
Venezuela	Polar		
Peru	CNC Backus		
Colombia	Bavaria Leona	Bavaria	SABMiller (acquired)

— Actual mergers   - - - Joint ventures

Source: Booz & Company

As the most successful Latin American brewers gained scale, they attracted the interest of brewers outside the region, such as Belgium's Interbrew and SAB (South African Breweries), which were aggressively acquiring companies in emerging markets, the former communist countries, and North America, where Interbrew acquired Labatt in Canada and SAB merged with U.S.-based Miller to form SABMiller. The regional strength of the Latin American brewers provided them with significant bargaining power and allowed them to generate substantial value for shareholders, as seen in Exhibit 4-5. Bavaria was sold to

EXHIBIT 4-5 SHAREHOLDER VALUE CREATED BY BAVARIA AND AMBEV

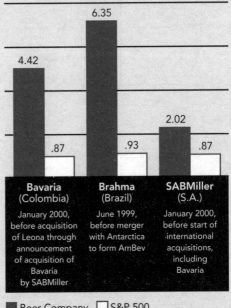

VALUE CREATION COMPARISON
(Value today of $1 invested in each company on . . .)

	Bavaria (Colombia)	Brahma (Brazil)	SABMiller (S.A.)
Beer Company	4.42	6.35	2.02
S&P 500	.87	.93	.87

Bavaria (Colombia): January 2000, before acquisition of Leona through announcement of acquisition of Bavaria by SABMiller

Brahma (Brazil): June 1999, before merger with Antarctica to form AmBev

SABMiller (S.A.): January 2000, before start of international acquisitions, including Bavaria

■ Beer Company   □ S&P 500

Notes:
1. Holding periods and local capital markets used:
Bavaria: 1/3/2000–6/30/2005 (14 days prior to acquisition by SABMiller; Bolsa de Valores de Colombia (BVC) since July 2001; Bogotá Stock exchange prior to July 2001
AmBev: 6/30/1999–12/31/2007; São Paulo Stock Exchange (BOVESPA)
SABMiller: 1/3/2000–12/31/2007; London Stock Exchange (LSE)
2. Values include the foreign exchange gain or loss against the U.S. dollar over the holding period for the Colombia peso, Brazilian real, and pound sterling.

Source: Booz & Company

SABMiller in exchange for stock, consolidating SAB-Miller's position at the time as the third-largest beer company in the world. Bavaria did not become a New

Blue in the purest sense of the word, but the Santo Domingo family, which controlled the company, became the second-largest shareholder of SABMiller after Altria, with significant representation on the board.

Only AmBev emerged as an independent global company. It merged with Interbrew to form InBev, the largest beer company in the world (in 2008, it announced that it would buy Anheuser-Busch). In addition to generating above-average returns, its global reach expanded to include 13 countries in the Americas and 32 countries worldwide. The CEO of AmBev was chosen as CEO of the new company InBev, and AmBev negotiated the same number of board seats as Interbrew. All of this made InBev a pathfinder that other New Blues will follow.

A NEW GAME FOR EMERGING MARKETS

Many of the current established blue chip companies—DuPont, ICI, GE, Procter & Gamble, IBM, Unilever—were founded during earlier waves of the Industrial Revolution. As they grew, they developed previously untapped markets in their home countries. They expanded rapidly to serve the fast-growing economies in North America and Europe, often relying primarily on organic growth. (In the United States in the early twentieth century, antitrust legislation had the effect of discouraging the use of M&A, particularly within single industries.) Today, the fast-developing economies in the New Blues' home countries are stimulating similar growth, but at a faster pace and with more M&A activity. This time, the New Blues are the companies that are leading the way. And this time, the main competitive field will probably be the emerging markets in which the New Blues were founded.

It will start with the "BRICs"—the acronym coined by Goldman Sachs to refer to Brazil, Russia, India, and China. For much of this decade, these four nations have enjoyed GDP growth of 7 percent or more per year, compared to less than 3 percent in most developed countries. China's growth is particularly significant; in 1987, its $268 billion GDP was the world's eleventh largest; in 2007, its GDP was $3.43 trillion, the world's fourth largest. Although BRIC growth rates have slowed since the meltdown of late 2008, they are still much higher than those of their European and North American counterparts.

The growth in the BRICs, and in developing economies in general, is not driven by exports alone, or even primarily; these countries also have fast-expanding middle classes. The middle-class population in Argentina, for instance, doubled from 2003 to 2007; Brazil's grew 50 percent from 2000 to 2005, and Mexico's grew by 88 percent from 1996 to 2006. India's middle-class population of 300 million already exceeds the population of both the United States and the European Union. These new middle classes are demanding a host of new products and services, forming what may well be tomorrow's most valuable consumer markets. Exhibit 4-6 shows a photograph of a new equity offering from the giant Indian real estate firm DLF, peddled next to a stall selling shoes. In 2007, the year this photograph was taken, India's fast-growing middle class helped propel the SENSEX, the Bombay Stock Exchange's

EXHIBIT 4-6 SIGNS OF A GROWING MIDDLE CLASS IN INDIA: A STOCK OFFERING

Source: Santosh Verma/*The New York Times*/Redux

30-share benchmark index, from 13,000 points to over 20,000 points.

The rise of the New Blues is happening in this context. They draw much of their power and capability from the rapid growth in their national markets. This synergy between market growth and New Blue corporate growth represents a defining trend that will influence M&A activity for the foreseeable future. The New Blues themselves stand to gain tremendously in this new world order. Meanwhile, leaders of traditional multinational companies from North America, Europe, and Japan face a new kind of challenge. The world was formerly their playground. Now they have a potent new set of competitors reaching the same new middle class of emerging global consumers, who are often very different from the consumers of more established industrial economies. The New Blues are increasingly visible in emerging markets themselves, competing with other companies to buy assets and build a presence. Chinese companies are making acquisitions throughout Asia, Latin America, and Africa; Brazilian companies increasingly seek to expand in Mexico, Central America, Colombia, Peru, and Argentina—and in Southeast Asia and China as well.

As they compete for M&A opportunities in emerging markets, the New Blues have several advantages: a financial muscle they never had before; direct experience with the consumers in their own regions; and a deep understanding of the economic patterns of emerging markets themselves.

This last point is critical. Just about every country in the world is evolving along a roughly similar developmental path. Though there are many variations, the path typically follows the same four stages in every country, based on the evolution of the prevailing population of consumers. In the first stage, most of the population is preoccupied with basic *survival*—obtaining adequate food, shelter, and clothing. In the second stage, a middle class begins to emerge, and people seek greater *quality* in the products and services that satisfy their basic needs. In the third stage, the middle class continues to grow, and, with the need for relatively high quality satisfied, people begin to seek *convenience*; they buy time-saving appliances and processed foods, and they may move closer to work. Finally, as the market graduates into the realm of developed nations, the population seeks *customization*; people will spend a premium to satisfy their individual tastes and desires.

By recognizing this general pattern, and identifying where a country currently fits into it, a company can plan its acquisitions more effectively. There are several key characteristics that provide clues to a country's progress along this path:

➤ *Infrastructure.* The extent, quality, and development of a country's roads, bridges, ports, and telecommunications—anything that supports the exchange of physical goods and data—is an important indicator of a country's development. India's road system, for example, has been severely neglected; traffic congestion, frequent checkpoints, and paperwork add hours to shipping. As a result, a trip across the country by truck that would take two days on a Western-style road system instead takes a week. It can also present a real risk to the cargo. For example, in some locations there aren't sufficient refrigerated vehicles to support a new prepared-foods strategy. Thus, strategically oriented companies will tend to buy assets that already have advantaged infrastructure or established local brand names. And in some cases, they might help to build infrastructure to support their expansion. We may see joint ventures in this domain, for example with public-sector or private-sector infrastructure.

➤ *Urbanization.* The proportion of the population living in or near cities is passing 50 percent for the first time in history, and this is extraordinarily significant for overall development. In nations with large rural populations, per capita income levels tend to be low, and reaching customers can add unanticipated expense to the cost of doing business. Conversely, in nations with large urban centers, these centers tend to stimulate sales of products and services. Urban families tend to have two incomes, with both adults working outside the home. They have more purchasing power, but also less time for food preparation and other household chores. Urban dwellers thus tend to buy more processed and prepared foods, and also to eat more meals outside the home. There is higher demand for personal-care products, such as shampoos, conditioners, and deodorants. Sales of durable goods, such as microwave ovens, refrigerators, and washing machines, rise too. In a country like China, where the population of urban dwellers grew by 350 million from 1980 to 2005, it's hard to overstate the impact of this trend on the fortunes of companies that choose to serve this market. The New Blues, in response, have moved beyond providing basic commodities and are seeking acquisitions that capture even more of the value-added business in their sectors.

➤ *Distribution channels.* As an economy evolves, so do the channels through which consumers purchase products, such as the retail format. Large retail formats have grown quickly in emerging markets; for instance, France's Carrefour SA has become the largest player in both Brazil and China. The local sales force and access to financing are also factors. The more expensive or complex the product that is being sold, the more sophisticated the sales force must be. Meanwhile, the availability of consumer credit can speed up sales of higher-ticket products as varied as automobiles, white goods, cell phones, and apparel. Distribution channels are particularly critical in M&A, because the growth of business depends on a viable value chain, and on the ability to franchise. New Blues' acquisitions abroad often target advantaged or hard-to-replicate distribution networks.

By understanding the natural development path of markets, both the New Blues and Western multinationals have a powerful way to increase the success rate of mergers and acquisitions in the emerging and developed markets. Deals that are properly aligned with an economy's development gain the added boost of favorable economic fundamentals; conversely, a deal that is mistimed and concluded at the wrong stage of a new market's development may fail no matter how advantageous its terms.

The BRIC countries and other emerging markets are rich territory that no multinational company can afford to ignore if it expects to prosper in this century. But these new markets also pose new challenges that require new merganic growth strategies, if only because of the level of global competition. If local governments in emerging economies tended to favor homegrown companies in the past, that tendency is limited now; companies from around the world are ready and able to enter these new markets quickly, often with equally facile skills. In fact, the distinction between "old" and "new" markets is blurring more quickly than ever. This means that the local and regional companies in these markets—those companies that are or aspire to be New Blues—don't have the luxury of depending on organic growth alone. They must attain scale quickly, using M&A and other deals even in their home and regional markets to win a share of the new business that is springing up around them. Emerging markets, in short, will become far more challenging business environments for both "old" and "new" blue chip companies.

Anheuser-Busch, which itself became the target of its larger overseas rival, InBev, was one company that successfully addressed the challenge of highly competitive emerging markets, generating international revenue growth of more than 400 percent from 1998 to 2007. The leading U.S. brewer, which reported $16.6 billion in 2007 revenues, typically expanded internationally by purchasing minority equity stakes in brewers in emerging markets or by creating joint ventures funded by cash, technology swaps, access to the company brands, and U.S. distribution deals. In return, Anheuser-Busch gained both access to new markets and more brands for its portfolio. In essence, the company applied "options" thinking to mergers and acquisitions.

Instead of a conventional market entry, which could have required a $2 billion initial investment, Anheuser-Busch created what amounted to call options on emerging markets. A relatively small investment enabled the company to test the waters, learn the local market, and refine the execution of its company strategy in that market before committing more capital. The smaller, discrete investments could be metered, subject to an ongoing evaluation of capital cost and availability, market opportunity, joint venture economics, and perceived risk. And if the investment appeared sound, Anheuser-Busch could "call" its option by buying out the remaining equity.

Minority investments and joint ventures also served as the equivalent of put options on local economies, allowing Anheuser-Busch to exit from those expansion opportunities that didn't pay off more easily and cost-effectively. It exercised these options with investments in Brazil and Chile. These forms of ownership limited the company's downside exposure to the initial option cost of a few million dollars; furthermore, the strategy created an opportunity for capital recovery (without creating a new entrant to the market) by selling back to the existing local partner, if required.

MASTERING SOFT POWER

Both New Blues and established multinationals from the West and elsewhere often have tremendous deal-making capacity. But although financial muscle and operational expertise are compulsory elements for M&A success, they are not adequate in and of themselves. Success also depends upon so-called soft power.

Joseph Nye, former dean of Harvard University's Kennedy School of Government, described the concept of *soft power* as a country's ability to gain geopolitical influence through culture or ideology, as opposed to military or financial might. Translated into business terms, soft power is a company's ability to attract and influence customers, employees, and, indeed, stakeholders of all kinds to make them want to participate in the company's mission and business activities.

The ability to wield soft power effectively is particularly important in a merger or acquisition. When the formal deal is complete, companies must find ways to motivate and inspire newly acquired workforces that are often as diverse in their cultural backgrounds as they are geographically. Harnessing soft power does not mean abandoning the culture on either side, but it requires a close look at the realities created by the deal and a deliberate discussion of the common aspirations, concerns, and behaviors that made those systems and cultures effective in the first place.

A few Japanese companies ignored soft power to their detriment in the 1980s and 1990s when they first expanded abroad. Leading Japanese securities firms Nomura and Daiwa, for instance, paid high salaries to attract and retain Western financial talent, but suffered high turnover costs because their new employees could not adjust to Japanese-style management.

Conversely, when SABIC acquired GE's plastics business, the Saudi chemical giant was buying an entirely new business and acquiring a large U.S. employee base along with it. This made talent retention a major consideration in the integration, a goal that required the adroit use of soft power. For instance, SABIC kept much of the existing leadership team in the plastics business intact.

"What makes [such integrations] work is treating people with respect and not coming in with a hatchet," says SABIC CFO Mutlaq H. Al-Morished. "You have to show them that you understand and appreciate the business and that you trust the people who operate the business. People are different. What works here in the Middle East doesn't necessarily work in Europe, and Europe is very different from the United States.

"A lot of mergers fail because the buying party tends to force its way of doing things on the other party. That's a big risk and it's not the way we work. We tend to do things slowly. We understand that acquired companies have something to offer us and that we can learn from them. Some of their practices are better than ours. Why shouldn't we take advantage of that? It has to be a two-way street."

Other companies have deployed soft power very well as their M&A efforts take them into developing nations. When Mittal Steel (now ArcelorMittal, the world's largest steelmaker) purchased a struggling steelmaker in Romania and was considering how to turn the business around, the chief financial officer, Aditya Mittal, received a most unusual piece of advice from the local Roman Orthodox bishop in the city where the target company was located. "You know," said the bishop, "the people have lost faith in this company; you need to rebuild their faith. Build a church at the entrance of your facility. Build a Roman Orthodox church. Get the workers to work with you to build it. You spend a couple million dollars and you build a beautiful church at the entrance to your facility. And I'm telling you that will work wonders."

The company took the bishop's advice. "We built a beautiful Roman Orthodox church; all the workers got involved in it part-time. And that changed every-thing," says Mittal, remembering how the integration barriers dropped away and the plant's workers embraced a new beginning. He credits this with part of the success that the company has had in Romania.

British bank Standard Chartered Group is another company that applies soft power in acquisions in developing nations. After purchasing Korea First Bank for $3.3 billion on April 15, 2005, Standard Chartered declared a "Korea Day" in all of its businesses around the world. "The aim of Korea Day is to welcome our colleagues in Korea First Bank into our international family," explained CEO Mervyn Davies. "It is also a day where we forge and initiate closer relationships and trade links across international boundaries with Korea. The sharing of best practice between our very enthusiastic and hugely talented Korean colleagues and others across the Standard Chartered global network will also figure prominently on Korea Day." The company repeated the exercise when it bought Hsinchu International Bank, a Taiwanese bank, in order to establish shared norms among multiple cultures.

However sophisticated they may be at using soft power and measured-entry tactics, established multinationals will face many new challenges in new markets. Through much of the twentieth century, global companies had a relatively clear playing field. The local companies in the new markets often couldn't provide the innovative, high-quality products that the newly prosperous local consumers were demanding, but the multinationals could. This is no longer the case; the New Blues can offer products and services that rival or even exceed those of established multinationals. So now, when multinationals arrive in a hot emerging market, odds are that New Blues are already sitting there or competing with them for entry. As a result, established multinationals need to rely on M&A and other partnerships to enter these markets rapidly enough to succeed there. Previous "go slow" organic efforts will not suffice.

In the short run, New Blues have other advantages. They are attuned not just to economic development but to political and regulatory considerations in emerging markets. They may also be favored by governments in their own home region. For example, in India the government has long upheld laws that protect local "mom and pop" retail stores by barring most foreign direct investment (though these restrictions are now easing). And China's lack of regulations on intellectual property and the environment, along with its labor laws, pose obstacles for companies looking to invest there.

The New Blues understand these dynamics, but established global companies may soon catch up; they too are eager to learn.

As the New Blues and the Old Blue Chips both gain in sophistication, the methods of competition will change. Some companies will become gifted at soft power. Others will gain prowess with global brands, or focus on cross-regional alliances. Still others, as management writer C. K. Prahalad suggests, may reduce the dominance of their home country and establish "hubs" around the world, with no fixed primary headquarters (HQ), but a virtual HQ composed of senior executives from a variety of regions. (Our own firm, Booz & Company, operates this way.) Leading companies will gain by copying the others' advantages; and those that are least constrained by their cultures and ways of thinking may be the companies that prevail.

5

PRIVATE EQUITY AND SOVEREIGN WEALTH

BACK IN MAY 2007, the $7.4 billion acquisition of Chrysler Group by the private equity firm Cerberus Capital Management was front-page news. One reason, of course, was the notoriety of the acquired company: an iconic American brand with a well-known and dramatic history. Chrysler had nearly gone bankrupt in 1977. It was saved by a 1979 government bailout, orchestrated with great fanfare by a highly visible and outspoken CEO, Lee Iacocca. Then it was targeted by the well-known investor Kirk Kerkorian; and merged, with great fanfare, with Daimler-Benz in 1998. Only nine years later, against the backdrop of a U.S. car industry reeling from rocketing gas prices, spiraling labor costs, and withering global competition, DaimlerChrysler admitted that the merger had failed and announced that it was selling an 80 percent stake in Chrysler to Cerberus. "Chrysler Deal Heralds New Direction for Detroit," announced the page one story in the *Wall Street Journal*.

Since that deal, of course, the notoriety has continued. The company has been through a credit collapse that hit the auto industry particularly hard, a multibillion-dollar U.S. government bailout, and a last-ditch alliance with Italy's Fiat. But Cerberus's purchase of Chrysler was noteworthy for another reason as well—as a harbinger of a significant new trend in the world of M&A. Rather than following the traditional "strip and flip" investment model for which private equity was often criticized, Cerberus declared that it was making a more permanent investment in the ailing carmaker, and with $26 billion in assets under management, the fund appeared to have the wherewithal to back up that claim. Then, instead of installing a CEO who was known for short-term turnarounds, Cerberus hired a top-ranked leader for Chrysler: Robert Nardelli, the former CEO of Home Depot and, before that, a long-time executive at General Electric, where he had been a contender to succeed Jack Welch.

"We don't think about the next quarter," said Cerberus chairman and former U.S. treasury secretary John Snow (shown with DaimlerChrysler CEO Dieter Zetsche in Exhibit 5-1). "We don't think about what analysts have to say about us. We care very much about producing long-term results for investors."

By early 2009, the Chrysler deal had not produced the long-term results for Cerberus investors that Snow envisioned. Indeed, Chrysler, along with much of the rest of

EXHIBIT 5-1 **DAIMLERCHRYSLER CEO DIETER ZETSCHE AND JOHN W. SNOW, CHAIRMAN OF CERBERUS CAPITAL MANAGEMENT LP (RIGHT), ANNOUNCE THE SALE OF CHRYSLER TO CERBERUS ON MAY 14, 2007**

Source: Myriam Vogel/AP Photo

the U.S.-based auto industry, is struggling to survive as we write this. But no matter what the final outcome for Cerberus and Chrysler, the trend in M&A will continue. Financial buyers and investors will act more and more like strategic buyers as time goes on.

These financial buyers come in many shapes and sizes, and their objectives vary widely. Some represent private equity (PE), including PE funds, infrastructure funds, and hedge funds. Cerberus is one example. Another is the consortium of PE firms, including Kohlberg Kravis Roberts & Co. (KKR), the Blackstone Group, and the Carlyle Group, which joined together to purchase VNU, now the Nielsen Co., in 2006. In this $12 billion deal, the consortium took the media firm private and tapped David Calhoun, a former vice chairman of General Electric, to be its CEO.

Other financial investors who are adopting a more strategy-oriented mindset include wielders of the wealth of nations: sovereign wealth funds (the government-controlled investment arms of cash-rich developing nations), the personal wealth funds of ruling families, and government-owned investment groups. A recession environment may encourage this trend. Middle East funds lost more than a quarter of their total value during 2008, and Chinese funds were buffeted by their exposure to the U.S. downturn. This has spurred many to shift their future focus from diverse, short-term financial plays to longer-term business-improvement-based vehicles and more concentrated investments.

The activity of financial buyers, especially sovereign wealth funds, hedge funds, and PE funds, slowed during the financial crisis of late 2008. For instance, between 2007 and 2008, the level of PE-led buyouts fell from 15 percent of all M&A activity to 6 percent. But financial buyers have by no means disappeared. Despite the temporary slowdown in deal making, PE firms continued to raise funds. Reports in early 2009 estimated that globally such firms have more than $1 trillion in capital available to make deals. They are also coping with recession and the disappearance of easy leverage by finding alternative means to participate in deals; for example, they are partnering with strategic buyers. Deals between strategic and financial buyers, for example, "private investment in public equity" ventures (known as PIPEs), had been unusual in the past, but they represent a creative response to the recession. Strategic buyers use PIPEs as an alternative source of deal funding in tight capital markets; financial buyers use them to take a long-term and advantaged equity position when they can no longer undertake high-leverage short-term deals on their own. With cash in hand and a strong motivation to invest, financial buyers will have a major and lasting impact on M&A in the future. They will continue to bolster deal activity and will push strategic buyers to develop more effective growth strategies and deal skills.

FINANCIAL BUYERS STEP UP

In a very real sense, Cerberus was a victim of its own success. It wouldn't have had the wherewithal to purchase Chrysler if it hadn't been so successful at delivering out-sized returns to its investors. In general, financial buyers as a whole have become a significant force in M&A because of their success at accumulating capital. For a variety of reasons, ranging from their ability to deliver high returns to low interest rates in developed economies to the price of oil, the investment capacity of financial buyers has grown to gargantuan levels, notwithstanding the setbacks of late 2008 and 2009. Given the vigorous competition for better returns by a larger number of capital sources, financial buyers have had to continually expand their search for viable investments, and they will remain aggressive in the acquisitions arena.

Private Equity

In the past five years, PE, hedge, and infrastructure funds have attracted capital from around the world, and some of them have grown to enormous proportions. In the United States, for example, PE firms Carlyle Group and Apollo

Management reported assets under management of over $82 billion and over $40 billion, respectively, in mid-2008.

The various types of private equity buyers raise money from a number of sources: institutions such as pension funds and insurance companies, endowments, high-net-worth individuals, and funds of funds. Many of these investors are reluctant to hold a direct investment in a private company; others are prohibited from doing so. But they can invest hundreds of millions of dollars—and pay a hefty management fee, typically 2 plus 20 (2 percent of assets under management and 20 percent of investment profits)—in a PE firm that can make a direct investment on their behalf.

The PE buyers' record of outsized returns is not the only reason that investors turn to them. They also invest because private equity firms' strategies differ from those of mutual funds and thus provide an important source of portfolio diversification. Yet another source of diversification is infrastructure funds, which buy stable, cash-flow-generating assets that support the operation of the economy, such as ports, airport authorities, and utilities. Infrastructure funds seek returns over a decade or more, PE funds think in terms of five-year plans for corporate turnarounds, and hedge funds hold minority stakes for shorter time frames, looking to flip their portfolios frequently.

Private equity and leveraged buyout deals have a history dating back well before the credit bubble. *Barbarians at the Gate: The Fall of RJR Nabisco* (published in 1990 by *Wall Street Journal* reporters Bryan Burrough and John Helyar) chronicled just such a deal that occurred in 1988, 20 years before the bubble. However, during the mid-2000s, the investor demand to participate in private equity vehicles increased significantly. In 2004, there were 26 investors in the average private equity fund; in 2006, the average had increased to 42 investors, according to Private Equity Intelligence Ltd. Many of these investors were high-net-worth individuals—those with over $1 million in assets—whose ranks swelled during this period. In 2006, according to a study by Capgemini and Merrill Lynch, there were 9.5 million of them worldwide, an 8.3 percent increase from 2005. Their combined wealth was $37.2 trillion, up 11.4 percent from 2005. The growth in numbers of these individuals has been especially striking in some emerging markets. Between 2005 and 2006, the United Arab Emirates' population of wealthy individuals rose 15.4 percent, Russia's rose 15.5 percent, Singapore's rose 21.3 percent, and India's rose 20.5 percent. In 2006, these wealthy individuals globally allocated 10 percent of their portfolios to alternative investments, including private equity.

When the subprime crisis began in 2007, PE-related fund-raising continued. As more and more investors funneled money into more and more private equity vehicles in pursuit of high returns and diversification, the M&A activity of private equity skyrocketed. "Private equity firms embarked on one of the biggest spending sprees in corporate history for nearly three years, using borrowed money to gobble up huge swaths of industries and some of the biggest names—Neiman Marcus, Metro-Goldwyn-Mayer and Toys "R" Us," began a November 2008 story in the *New York Times*. A study of more than 21,000 private equity transactions between 1970 and 2007 by the World

Economic Forum found that 40 percent of those transactions occurred after January 2004. The total value of those deals was estimated at $3.6 trillion, of which $2.7 trillion occurred between 2001 and 2007. As a result, at the beginning of 2007, close to 14,000 firms worldwide were held by private equity groups, as opposed to fewer than 5,000 in 2000 and fewer than 2,000 in the mid-1990s.

Then, in the latter half of 2008, the M&A activity of private equity fell substantially with the financial shake-up. The leverage that many PE funds depended upon to buy companies disappeared as banks stopped lending. Investors deserted hedge funds as the equity markets shrank, forcing some funds to sell out their positions. But it is clear, nonetheless, that like the financial markets themselves, the fundamentals and activity levels of this set of buyers will return to the norm, rather than disappear. The vast amount of capital, currently waiting to reenter once there is some assurance that the markets will function normally again, virtually guarantees that private equity–based M&A and hedge fund investing are here to stay.

National Wealth

The wealth generated in developing nations, especially in the Middle East and Asia, is further swelling the ranks of financial buyers. On the heels of globalization and the long bull market in commodities, these buyers, which include the investment funds of nations, wealthy families, and state-owned companies, are very well endowed.

Sovereign wealth funds are estimated to control between $2 and $3.3 trillion in assets, a number that analysts predict will balloon to $12 trillion by 2015. Record oil

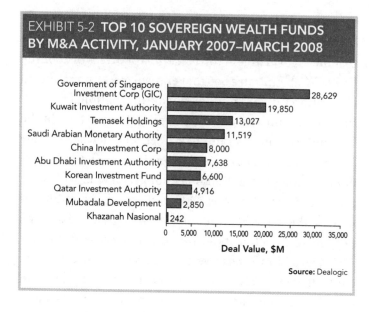

EXHIBIT 5-2 **TOP 10 SOVEREIGN WEALTH FUNDS BY M&A ACTIVITY, JANUARY 2007–MARCH 2008**

Government of Singapore Investment Corp (GIC) — 28,629
Kuwait Investment Authority — 19,850
Temasek Holdings — 13,027
Saudi Arabian Monetary Authority — 11,519
China Investment Corp — 8,000
Abu Dhabi Investment Authority — 7,638
Korean Investment Fund — 6,600
Qatar Investment Authority — 4,916
Mubadala Development — 2,850
Khazanah Nasional — 242

Deal Value, $M

Source: Dealogic

prices have filled the coffers of sovereign wealth funds in Kuwait, Saudi Arabia, Dubai, Abu Dhabi, and Qatar with about $1.5 trillion in assets. This, in turn, has stimulated these funds' investing activity. In the first three quarters of 2007, these five Middle Eastern funds invested $64 billion globally, compared to $30.8 billion in all of 2006 and $4.5 billion in 2004.

Sovereign wealth funds have traditionally behaved as passive investors, often investing through financial firms, increasing their exposure and looking for near-term arbitrage plays. But as shown in Exhibit 5-2, they are increasingly buying direct stakes in companies, or even making outright acquisitions. Government-owned entities headquartered in developing nations have also become more active M&A players, especially as the nations where they are headquartered lower trade and regulatory barriers and they must attain scale to compete. Since 2006, for instance, government-owned Dubai Ports World of the United Arab Emirates bought Peninsular & Oriental Steam Navigation Co., of London; Dubai International Capital, the investment arm of Dubai's ruling family, bought the Tussauds Group, operator of attractions such as Madame Tussauds wax museums; and sovereign wealth fund Kingdom Holdings of Saudi Arabia (along with Microsoft's Bill Gates and Four Seasons CEO and founder Izzy Sharp) bought the Four Seasons hotel chain. When Barclay's needed to sweeten its ultimately unsuccessful bid for ABN Amro, the China Development Bank, a government-controlled lender, offered to invest between €2.2 billion and €9.8 billion, and Singapore sovereign investment fund Temasek Holdings pledged as much as €3.6 billion. After the late 2008 economic shock, even when these funds look for passive investments, they are seeking more focused strategic plays with longer time horizons. They are turning more to strategic partners than to financial managers.

National wealth investors are looking East as well as West, adding to the competitive pressure for acquisitions in some of the fastest-developing economies in the world. Dubai International Capital, for example, had invested more than $1 billion in Asia by late 2007 and announced plans to invest an additional $2.5 billion in India and China—particularly in the areas of manufacturing, real estate, and finance. It took a large stake in Bank of China and Malaysia's Bank of Islam; in India, it invested in the real estate developer DLF Ltd. and travel service provider Thomas Cook. Meanwhile, Temasek Holdings and the

Government of Singapore Investment Corp. announced that they would double their combined stake in India's ICICI Bank.

Through the Crisis

The breadth of activity on the part of financial buyers of all kinds reinforces the idea that the global M&A environment will continue to be active and will become more competitive than ever before. With so much capital to deploy, financial buyers are inevitably considering a broader range of targets—and the downturn is providing them with an assortment as companies go on the auction block. PE firms are returning to their roots, providing longer-term investments in distressed companies, such as the April 2008 refinancing of troubled thrift Washington Mutual, Inc. (WaMu). In this case, WaMu declined an all-stock takeover offer from JPMorgan Chase & Co. and bypassed reported interest from Wells Fargo, accepting instead a capital infusion of $7 billion from TPG, Inc., a major U.S. PE firm. In return, TPG became a majority shareholder in the troubled company, receiving a seat on the board and a 13 percent stake in discounted stock.

Not all the members of the new wave of financial buyers will survive the meltdown unscathed. In late September 2008, TPG reported losing $1.35 billion on its investment in WaMu after U.S. regulators seized the thrift and sold its branch operations to JPMorgan for $1.9 billion. Some of the Middle East sovereign wealth funds have also seen the value of their stakes in the struggling Wall Street firms quickly dwindle. And in China, the first investment made by the government's new $200 billion overseas investment fund, a $3 billion stake in the Blackstone Group made in 2007, lost $425 million in six weeks. This produced an unusual public backlash from individual Chinese citizen bloggers and even some Chinese media figures, who complained that the government had been duped.

"O senior officials of the Chinese government," complained one anonymous writer on the Chinese Web site Sina.co, referring to the Blackstone investment, "please do not be fooled by sweet-talking wolves dressed in human skin. The foreign reserves are the product of the sweat and blood of the people of China, please invest them with more care!" In January 2008, the Chinese government quashed the China Development Bank's plan to invest $2 billion in Citigroup, a sign of the pressures that sovereign wealth fund managers are facing if they don't deliver performance.

But having been tested by market turbulence and the complexities of the M&A environment, financial buyers will remain formidable competitors. They will be more competent in gauging risk and more resilient in their approaches than they have been in the past.

A GLOBAL ROLE FOR FINANCIAL BUYERS

Even as they invest in the developed nations, financial buyers are also increasingly active in emerging markets. This represents a sea change from years past. As Exhibit 5-3 shows, in the 30 years from 1970 to 2000, the percentage of all private equity activity in the United States was 55.1 percent of the global total. In the 2001–2007 time

EXHIBIT 5-3 GEOGRAPHIC DISTRIBUTION OF PE TRANSACTIONS, 1970–2000 AND 2001–2007

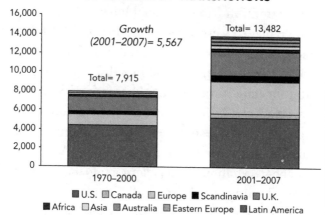

GLOBAL DISTRIBUTION OF PRIVATE EQUITY BY NUMBER OF TRANSACTIONS

Growth (2001–2007)= 5,567

Total= 7,915

Total= 13,482

1970–2000 2001–2007

■ U.S. ■ Canada ■ Europe ■ Scandinavia ■ U.K. ■ Africa ■ Asia ■ Australia ■ Eastern Europe ■ Latin America

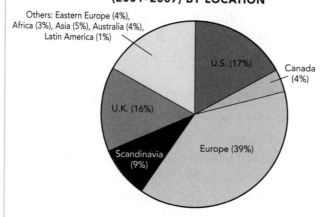

% SHARE OF GROWTH IN PE TRANSACTIONS (2001–2007) BY LOCATION

Others: Eastern Europe (4%), Africa (3%), Asia (5%), Australia (4%), Latin America (1%)

U.S. (17%)

Canada (4%)

U.K. (16%)

Scandinavia (9%)

Europe (39%)

Source: World Economic Forum, 2007; Booz Allen

period, that majority share slipped to 34.8 percent. India alone saw total investment increase 700 percent between 2004 and 2006, from $1.1 billion to $7.5 billion.

Given the economic growth rates of many Asian nations, it is not surprising that this region is attracting greater attention from financial buyers. In 2007, U.S.-based PE players were expected to add about $25 billion in the second half of 2007; that second-half figure was up 57 percent from the same period in 2006, according to the Center for Asia Private Equity Research. U.S.-based PE players KKR and TPG, Inc., launched $4 billion and $4.2 billion Asia funds, respectively, and CVC Capital Partners in Luxembourg signed commitments for an Asia fund totaling about $5 billion. Even Japan got into the act. In 2007, Nomura Holdings and Norinchukin Bank created Japan's first major asset-management firm specializing in private equity investments. Nomura also announced that it was planning a PE fund with an exclusively Asian focus. And, in early 2009, cash-flush Japanese companies that view the recession as a buying opportunity were also attracting the interest of regional PE funds, such as Barings Private Equity Asia K.K., which see these companies as deal-making partners.

Another sign of the long-term strength of Eastern economies is the emergence of private equity funds within China itself, where Western firms are often blocked by the government from investing. In 2006, China's government approved the Bohai Industrial Investment Fund Management Co., managed by Bank of China Ltd.'s investment-banking arm, specifically to compete with the foreign private equity firms. Near the end of 2007, the Bohai Fund paid $135 million for a stake in Chengdu City Com-

mercial Bank, an industry that foreigners have had difficulty tapping.

In the same vein, in early 2008, Fang Fenglei, a Chinese deal maker with ties to Goldman Sachs, set up the $2
billion private equity Hopu Fund. Goldman planned to put
around $300 million into the Hopu Fund as a limited part-
ner, but about half of the cash, roughly $1 billion, was to
come from Singapore's Temasek Holdings. Concurrently,
Fang set up a separate domestic yuan-denominated fund
in the city of Suzhou in eastern China. That fund, called the
China-Singapore High-Tech Industrial Investment Fund,
planned to raise 5 billion yuan, or close to $700 million.

Said David Rubenstein, cofounder of the Carlyle Group,
in 2007: "You'll see our biggest competition will not be
from one another, but will be from the indigenous Chinese
private equity firms that have many strengths that we just
can't possibly have."Rubenstein is right in assessing the
competitive strength of Chinese private equity, but in
the long run, the nationality of the investors' firms may not
be the most critical factor. Asian, American, European,
and other financial buyers will all be looking for opportunities around the world. They'll all have developed—or
bought—the expertise they need to become global financial players.

STRATEGIC
DEVELOPMENT
ON THE RISE

As the buying power of financial deal makers grows larger
and expands globally, the very nature of their role in the

M&A universe is changing. Traditionally, as their name implies, these buyers thought about acquisitions solely in financial terms and typically resold companies in a three-to five-year time frame. Value was derived principally through a change in leadership, cost cutting, and head-count reductions. Financial buyers also sought to minimize their own investment by borrowing as much as possible.

What role will financial buyers play in the future? They will continue to compete with strategic buyers for deals, but they also may increasingly join with them as buying partners. Witness the growing use of PIPEs to finance deals and the interest in teaming up with Japanese companies. These buyers may also become sellers, to the extent that they cannot or do not want to continue to own the many companies they have acquired in recent years. And finally, they will also be fiercer competitors for customers and talent as they develop the deep operational expertise needed to extract value from their investments.

Indeed, private equity firms are increasingly going beyond changes in leadership, headcounts, organizational charts, and balance sheets. They are strategically repositioning the companies that they buy and improving their operational execution. One sign of this growing emphasis on strategic development is the lengthening timelines on PE acquisitions. In the 1990–1994 time frame, 37 percent of the companies acquired by PE firms were sold within four years. In the 2003–2005 time frame, this figure dropped to 23 percent. (These figures are traditional private equity deals only and do not include leveraged management buyouts.)

LITTLE SHEEP'S BIG LEAP

The relationship between 3i, a U.K.-based PE firm, and Little Sheep, a rapidly growing Chinese restaurant chain, shows how some PE firms are adopting a more strategic orientation to create value.

In August 1999, an entrepreneur named Zhang Gang founded Little Sheep Catering Chain Co. in Inner Mongolia. His first restaurant offered a version of the local "hot pot" dish, where thinly sliced lamb is dipped into a flavored soup. The restaurant proved to be such a success that Zhang opened two more restaurants two months later. The chain grew rapidly, adding both chain-owned and franchised restaurants. By 2004, Little Sheep had joined the ranks of the "Top 500 Enterprises of China." By 2005, Zhang was contemplating an IPO.

Not surprisingly, Little Sheep's extraordinary growth attracted many willing investors, but the company chose 3i. Critical to this choice was 3i's underlying investment philosophy, which included People's Programmes, a network of seasoned executives and industry experts who evaluate and assist in its investments; and the Business Development Practice, a dedicated team that helps 3i's portfolio companies expand their operations internationally.

For Little Sheep, the 3i team tapped Nish Kankiwala, former president of Burger King International, as a suitable advisor. When Kankiwala flew to Beijing to meet with the chain's executives, it was the first time they had had direct access to an expert with a deep understanding of their business and franchising. That connection helped cinch the deal, and after making a $25 million equity investment in the company in late 2005, the 3i team helped Little Sheep's management create a 180-day plan that kicked into gear as soon as the transaction closed in mid-2006. This plan included strengthening the management team and board by recruiting additional professional managers, installing management information systems, enhancing the communication and coordination among Little Sheep's three regional operations, creating and executing a new franchise strategy that focused on quality rather than quantity, and strengthening domestic operations before pursuing overseas expansion.

Early results from this restructuring have been promising. Between the time the 3i transaction closed in mid-2006 and the end of 2007, Little Sheep closed stores that were performing poorly, opened 37 new stores, and achieved year-on-year growth of 40 percent, far ahead of the 15 to 20 percent growth in China's food sector. By mid-2008, Little Sheep had 326 restaurants covering 34 provinces in China. Additionally, there were also Little Sheep restaurants in the United States, Japan, and Canada. In March 2009, the U.S. restaurant operator Yum! Brands—owners of the KFC, Pizza Hut, and Taco Bell chains—announced that it was buying a 20 percent stake in

Little Sheep for $63 million, much of it from 3i. The private equity firm reportedly trebled its original investment through this sale.

The financial buyers' growing commitment to the new modus operandi around strategic development is also evidenced by their stepped-up recruitment of executives with operational experience in specific industries. These executives help in finding and researching deals, recruiting other executives, counseling managers, and sometimes running the acquired companies.

Cerberus had former Chrysler Group operating chief Wolfgang Bernhard advising it on its acquisition of Chrysler. Kenneth W. Freeman, former CEO of Quest Diagnostics Inc., is now working for two KKR-backed companies: he is CEO of door-maker Masonite and executive chairman of the medical-device firm Accellent. Former GE CEO Jack Welch is a special partner at Clayton, Dubilier & Rice, and former IBM CEO Louis V. Gerstner Jr. is chairman of the Carlyle Group.

Big pay is one lure for the executives who are recruited by private equity firms. Another is the opportunity to work without public scrutiny by the analysts and investors whom they often faced when at publicly traded companies. Also, because of the number of companies in which many private equity firms have stakes, there are more opportunities for a recruited executive to serve as CEO, a career goal that can be elusive when an executive is employed in one company.

Financial buyers may not be able to obtain the operational scale advantages of strategic buyers, but by enlisting the best and the brightest executives and giving them the proper time and resources to operate an acquired company, significant profits are possible. A good example is the leveraged buyout of Dubai-based transportation and logistics services provider Aramex, the first Arab company to be listed on the Nasdaq, by Abraaj Capital, a Dubai PE firm, in 2002. Abraaj teamed up with Aramex founder and CEO Fadi Ghandour, who continues to lead the company today, to create value through a new ESOP-based incentive plan, strategic acquisitions, reduced overhead, and the expansion of existing services to new customers. Within the next two years, Aramex's net profits grew 196 percent. In June 2005, the company launched its IPO on the Dubai Financial Market, and Abraaj earned an internal rate of return of 74 percent on its investment.

Innovation can be enhanced as well as profits. The World Economic Forum found one measure of the degree of innovation at companies under the purview of a private equity buyer: patent citations. Of the 500 companies studied, patent citations increased 25 percent after the companies' acquisition by PE firms. The conclusion: "Private equity-backed firms concentrated on core technologies. The increase in patent importance, as denoted by patent citations, is greatest in the patent classes where the firm has had its historic focus and where it increases its activities after the private equity investment." The number of patents is not always a reliable indicator of good financial results from innovation, but in this context it shows that private equity firms are willing to invest in expanded

R&D—another sign of their interest in improving the quality of management in general.

HERE TO STAY

The growth of financial buyers and their shift toward a more strategic orientation means that they must expand their M&A activities and managerial competencies. In the past, these buyers could often depend on cost cutting and balance sheet management to allow them to turn a tidy profit from the sale of a recently acquired company. But when financial buyers become long-term business operators, they must invest more time and money, provide more operational expertise, and often make substantive changes at the acquired company before they can hope to resell it. Like any corporation running a business unit, they must be able to identify and correct operational and management weaknesses, coax structural changes, revamp strategy, and identify opportunities to reposition a company in its industry.

Corporations, the traditional strategic buyers, are also affected by the shifting role and greater participation of financial buyers in M&A. As the acquisition range of financial buyers grows, so does the level of competition for deals. As financial buyers build their operating expertise and raise the level of their management teams, the level of market competition increases within industries. Furthermore, operations-based deal synergies are no longer the sole province of corporate buyers, as acquisitions by financial buyers may now lead to larger portfolios in newly merged companies. For example, the Blackstone Group and Wellspring Capital Management Food announced in January 2008 that they would buy food distributor Performance Food Group Co. for about $1.3 billion and combine it with Vistar Corp., a food-service distributor that they already controlled, solidifying their position as the third-largest company in the food-supplier industry, behind Sysco Corp. and U.S. Foodservice Inc.

In short, the investors from private equity and national wealth funds are no longer niche M&A players. In the short term, the overheated levels of deals driven by financial buyers will continue to fall from their recent peaks, and these buyers will adjust their business models to compensate for their lack of leverage. Over the long term, they are, and will continue to be, in hot pursuit of acquisitions around the world. These players still have trillions of dollars to invest, which means that M&A will be more competitive than ever, and that doing deals successfully will be more essential than ever. The strategic buyers of the future will find themselves fighting a multipronged battle, competing with financial buyers who are acting more and more strategically in the quest for attractive assets and talent.

6

BUBBLES
AND WAVES

AS THE CREDIT CRISIS and subsequent recession brought down financial markets and spread across national economies late in 2008, many observers proclaimed that M&A was dead. They reasoned that the bank failures, the disappearance of credit, fleeing investors, and frightened consumers would hasten and aggravate the recessionary trend and simply quash deal making. However, they were incorrect in their conclusion that M&A activity would come to a standstill. What these observers missed was the distinction between *bubbles*, such as the speculative rise in the U.S. housing market that was a core cause of the financial crisis, and *waves*, or long-term trends such as those discussed in the previous four chapters. It's the waves, not the bubbles, that drive M&A activity overall, while the perception of bubbles may serve as either a transient spur or a temporary brake to M&A momentum.

There is no doubt that the financial crisis slowed down M&A activity to a significant extent at first. Dealogic reported that October 2008 set a record for scuttled deals—134 deals valued at $118 billion were withdrawn. And although the overall deal volume of $451.5 billion in that month was the highest monthly volume since November 2007, the number is deceptively large, since it includes $242.5 billion in government activity—mainly stakes taken in financial institutions to stabilize the global economy. In fact, according to a Booz & Company analysis, the total number of deals closed in the fourth quarter of 2008 was 2,996. This represented a 58 percent decline from the fourth quarter of 2007. Comparing the same two periods, total deal value in the fourth quarter of 2008 declined 44 percent to $610 billion.

However, even with the elevated heights of uncertainty and turmoil, traditional strategic buyers, New Blues, and various financial players are and will continue to be active M&A players. In October 2008, for instance, Delta Air Lines' $2.8 billion acquisition of Northwest Airlines closed, a deal that created the world's biggest airline carrier and is expected to set off a wave of scale-driven M&A throughout the industry. Also, the diversified mining company Teck Cominco Ltd. closed its $14 billion acquisition of Fording Canadian Coal Trust, and rural telephone company CenturyTel, Inc., announced a $5.8 billion all-stock deal for its larger competitor Embarq Corporation.

Nor did the financial buyers disappear completely, although their activity levels in 2008, especially among private equity (PE) firms, sank by more than 90 percent compared to a year earlier. In October 2008, the Blackstone Group closed its $1.6 billion acquisition of home-health-care services company Apria Healthcare Group, the U.K.-based PE firm Duke Street completed the $271 million acquisition of French medical diagnostics company Biomnis, and the Carlyle Group completed its plans to acquire the U.K. aerospace supplier Gardner Group for an undisclosed amount that is estimated to be about $83 million.

The many buying opportunities among distressed companies will also raise the activity levels of financial buyers. In late 2008 and early 2009, numerous PE firms announced their intentions to pursue such targets. In January 2009, a consortium of private equity firms and hedge funds agreed to pay $13.9 billion for failed lender IndyMac Bank; the PE firm Golden State Capital took an unsuccessful run at bankrupt big box retailer Circuit City and announced it was targeting acquisitions in the hard-hit building products sector; and a variety of sovereign wealth funds and leading PE firms—such as the Carlyle Group, the TPG Group, and KKR—were reported to be preparing competing bids for International Lease Finance, AIG's aircraft leasing unit and the owner of $55 billion worth of planes.

While the multibillion-dollar PE-driven deals of past years have certainly shrunk (the Carlyle Group's $2.5 billion purchase of a majority stake in Booz Allen Hamilton's U.S. government consulting business was one of the larger PE deals in the second half of 2008), it may be, as Carlyle Group cofounder David Rubenstein suggested in March 2008, that the "greatest period for private equity" still lies ahead. Of course, Rubenstein made sure to temper his statement with a cautionary note. "During this period of time," he added, "probably for the next year or so, you'll see much smaller deals done. The large deals won't get done because there's nobody to syndicate those deals. Secondly, you'll see non-leveraged deals where people take minority stakes but they don't use leverage as much. And you'll see much more overseas activity from the private equity firms in places such as China or India where leverage in many private equity transactions is not quite as important."

Rubenstein's pessimism, based on credit markets that had already begun to freeze up in late 2007, was prescient. But in the long term, his optimism will probably prove just as accurate. M&A will weather the economic storm because it is undertaken by a diverse group of players, some of whom do not depend on the capital markets as much as others do. For instance, all the signs suggest that strategic M&A activity will continue to be strong, both because of the opportunity created by private equity retrenchment and, more importantly, because the leverage levels of corporations in many sectors are low and many companies are flush with cash. Furthermore, the case for strategic deals remains strong; underlying economic and sector drivers are powering waves of consolidation.

In early November 2008, for example, Japanese consumer electronics giant Panasonic agreed to acquire its competitor Sanyo by year-end in a deal valued at $8 to $9 billion in order to gain relevant scale. In January 2009, Pfizer announced it would acquire Wyeth to build its capabilities in biologics and replenish its product pipeline. Merck followed in March with a $41 billion offer for Schering-Plough. Other deals were attempted in the agriculture sector (driven by consolidation) and in medical devices and technology (seeking growth-based add-ons).

ANATOMY OF A CYCLE

Mergers and acquisitions are often driven by the perception that an economic or market wave is beginning: an enduring shift in the fundamentals of industries. But it is not
always easy to tell a wave from a bubble: a short-term surge
that often occurs on top of a wave and causes the wave to
break. For investors and acquirers alike, therefore, the
ability to distinguish a wave from a bubble is paramount.
Many of the megadeals of the mid-2000s had rationales
based on expected returns from a wave that, in reality,
turned out to be a bubble. The expected results failed to
materialize after the bubble burst. Deals premised on
bubble-based rationales often fail, as the underlying
forces enabling or supporting the transactions disappear.
Conversely, deals that are passed up because a wave is mis-
taken for a bubble can involve huge lost opportunity costs,
especially when competitors ride the wave successfully.

While there are important distinctions between bubbles and waves, they are easily confused. Often, both are
defined by the same activity indicators: the volume (or ag-
gregate prices of companies bought), the number of deals
per month or per year, and the valuations, in terms of
share price as a multiple of earnings, of companies purchased at the time. The rise and fall of these indicators
gives a wave, or a bubble, its shape. And at certain stages
of their life cycles, the two phenomena have very similar
shapes; they look and feel the same. For instance, in the
initial stages of both bubbles and waves, deal prices rise
and there is strong buyer interest; the marketplace becomes frothy. They both act as accelerants that open the
door to a flood of investment and rapidly create a level of

development that normally would have taken a much longer time. But the underlying dynamics of waves and bubbles are quite distinct, even when they are intertwined.

In the U.S. economy over the past five decades, a series of waves and bubbles have risen together. Typically the wave rises slowly (as measured, for example, in gross domestic product activity); then the bubble rises and crashes more visibly. (The bubble's activity can best be measured by the number of deals or the average amount spent in M&A; the wave's activity tends to correlate more with the overall performance of the economy.) Four separate waves and bubbles in the United States, echoed in corresponding rises in M&A activity, over the past 45 years are shown in Exhibit 6-1. The wide bars are waves; the rising peaks in M&A deal counts or dollar amounts represent the much more abrupt bubbles that followed and broke the wave, only to be replaced by a new wave, gradually building.

When you look at this pattern over time, one characteristic is particularly relevant to M&A: the increasing frequency and amplitude of the bubbles (and their accompanying waves as well). The first wave-and-bubble pair shown on this timeline occurred in the mid- to late 1960s, when companies responded to "go-go" equity markets and antitrust regulations with a wave of diversification. It was more than a decade before the next major wave-and-bubble pair in the United States occurred. It lasted from 1981 to 1987, and increased M&A activity was driven this time by financial buyers who had mastered the leveraged buyout; by foreign buyers, notably from Japan and the United Kingdom; and, again, by a fast-rising stock market. The next pair started just five years later; this time the rise in

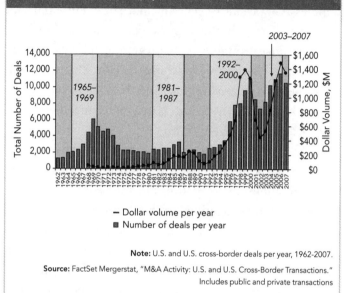

EXHIBIT 6-1 **M&A ACTIVITY IN BUBBLES AND WAVES IN THE UNITED STATES, 1962–2007**

— Dollar volume per year
■ Number of deals per year

Note: U.S. and U.S. cross-border deals per year, 1962-2007.

Source: FactSet Mergerstat, "M&A Activity: U.S. and U.S. Cross-Border Transactions."
Includes public and private transactions

M&A was driven by the federal deregulation of the broadcasting, telecommunications, health-care, and banking sectors, and the rise of the Internet. Finally, just three years after that, another pair formed, driven by easy credit and globalization. As in the past, M&A acivity followed as financial buyers came to the fore and strategic buyers strove to gain access to emerging markets and also to gain scale.

Similar patterns can be seen in other regions, such as Europe, and they have been noted by other observers (for example, by Robert J. Borghese of the Wharton School and his coauthor Paul Borgese, in their book *M&A from Planning to Integration*). This increasing frequency and amplitude is an enduring trend that will shape the future of global M&A. It is enduring because it is a natural by-product of the four trends discussed in the preceding chapters. Bubbles and waves are occurring more frequently and with greater intensity because more companies are seeking scale, because capital moves with greater velocity and impatience, and because of the competitive intensity brought on by the rise of the New Blues and the deep pockets of financial buyers. The net result is increasing turbulence and risk within the M&A environment.

Adding to the challenge of deciphering the environment is that a bubble and a wave often influence each other's momentum, propelling and then constraining demand and prices together. In the 1990s, while the stock bubble in "New Economy" dot-com companies pushed M&A to an unsustainable level, it too was pushed forward by the underlying Internet adoption wave. The credit bubble that peaked in mid-2007 in the United States provides a converse example. Interest rates on the high-yield bonds that often fund acquisitions dipped to a record low of 2.63 percentage points above Treasury bonds in June, about half the 20-year historic average of 5.4 percent. It is now clear that less-than-sound M&A deals were made during that bubble, and that the bursting of the bubble temporarily put a halt to the underlying consolidation wave.

This puts more pressure than ever on executives to create and execute sound, responsive growth strategies. A wave, when seen, presents a historic opportunity and can power a company's long-term strategy; a bubble is more likely to be a trap baited with short-term profits. To navigate in frothy times, executives must understand the true nature of the business environment, asking themselves: "Is my industry in the midst of a bubble or a wave?" "Am I faced with an opportunity to grow the business, or am I being tempted by a deal that will destroy value?"

Then, having distinguished wave opportunities from bubble-driven dangers, executives must also have the fortitude to stand by their conclusions even when everyone else seems to be reaping rewards. The leaders of Wells Fargo and JPMorgan Chase remained true to their course during the credit wave and bubble of 2008. Their companies emerged among the few major healthy banks left in the U.S. financial sector (prior to the Wells Fargo-Wachovia merger).

WHAT IS A WAVE?

Waves tend to begin when there is a permanent or semipermanent shift in the balance between supply and demand, typically when a new technology has emerged or there has been a change in customer needs, tastes, or demographics. In short, something intrinsic has changed in the environment, affecting supply or demand in a fundamental way. There are many waves under way at any given time. Recent waves can be traced to many factors: the advances in genetics that spurred R&D-driven deals in the biotechnology industry in the 1990s; the lowering of global trade barriers, which has enticed industries as diverse as mining companies and beer makers to reach out for new markets; and the deregulation in the U.S. banking, telecom, and utility industries, which created a wave of acquisitions and mergers.

Other causes of waves might include changes in the capital markets, such as the opening of China's economy;

commodity shortages and price shocks (as long as they are long-lasting enough to produce major shifts in behavior); tax changes (though tax-related waves are less enduring than other waves, since governments change tax rules frequently); and demographic changes, such as large-scale migration to cities in many developing nations.

There are two major precepts to follow for companies that hope to ride an M&A wave. First, participate in the wave as early as possible. Do not be deterred by the fast rise in prices that occurs during a fundamental transformation. At least one academic study has shown that companies that act on a wave early earn much greater returns than companies led by more cautious or less observant executives.

The study examined 3,194 public companies in 12 industries during acquisition waves between 1984 and 2004. The researchers defined a merger wave as occurring when the peak year had a greater than 100 percent increase in activity from the first year, followed by a decline in acquisition activity of greater than 50 percent from the peak year. They found that the share prices of companies doing deals in the first 15 percent of a consolidation wave tended to increase by a greater percentage, when measured against the performance of the broad market. Shares of companies that were latecomers to the deal-making surge fell an average of 3 percent.

Second—and this is as important as acting quickly—companies that want to ride a wave must ensure that the valuations they are considering remain tethered to the underlying fundamentals of the change. A wave has to support a company's strategic direction (for example, the wave of M&A that follows deregulation) or lead to a sober reassessment of strategy before riding the wave is justifiable.

In other words, prospective acquirers must avoid being swept away with the herd when demand rises, velocity and impatience add to the urgency, and the bubble mentality takes hold. They must also remain disciplined in their assumptions about the future. There is always a temptation to overestimate synergies and other outcomes in order to justify a desirable deal, but when those estimates do not materialize, mergers and acquisitions fail.

WHAT IS A BUBBLE?

Broadly defined, an M&A bubble is a surge in prices brought about by a temporary spike in demand that far exceeds the available supply. Often this demand reflects an inaccurate perception of rapid returns, which in turn triggers emotionally driven surges in investment that reinforce the perception, creating what former Federal Reserve Chairman Alan Greenspan famously termed "irrational exuberance." Since it is unwarranted by the business fundamentals, this demand surge eventually becomes unsustainable, leading to a drastic price drop and sell-off. The pattern has been observed in print for decades, going back to Charles Mackay's 1841 classic, *Extraordinary Popular Delusions and the Madness of Crowds*, which used it to explain the Dutch tulip craze of the 1600s, the South Sea Bubble of the early 1700s, and the popularity of alchemy before them.

Bubbles can be, and often are, powered initially by some intrinsic and permanent change in the business environment, but as more investors and more diverse players pile on in search of quick returns, the bubble quickly outruns the normal pace of change. As prices surpass the fundamentals that initially stimulated them, they gain momentum from other less-sustainable sources of activity. The surge in prices becomes the driver of action rather than a measured response to the reality.

Sources of momentum include the herd mentality, rumors and other misinformation (or incomplete information), and the influence of money gluts. The frequency and severity of today's bubbles are abetted by a flood of global savings. Global central bank reserves surged to a record $6.4 trillion in the last quarter of 2007, up from $4 trillion in 2005, according to the International Monetary Fund. A lot of those savings have gone into ultra-safe U.S. Treasury bonds. Foreigners held $2.32 trillion of these bonds at the end of 2007, compared to $1.98 trillion in 2005. That intense demand for Treasury bonds, the weakness in the U.S. dollar, and the Fed's cutting of interest rates drove down yields and forced investors to search for better returns elsewhere. With so much savings looking for higher yields, a rush into and out of investments that promise greater returns was inevitable, pumping up and deflating prices.

How does one recognize a bubble? Identifying bubbles is not easy, and experts have failed miserably at it throughout history—remember the calls in 2000 for Dow 20,000 or predictions in mid-2008 that oil would reach $200 per barrel? Nevertheless, and without being glib, there is a certain degree of common sense involved.

One sign of a bubble is that valuations break free from historical norms, sometimes becoming so unhinged that companies, analysts, and the media invent new metrics to explain why things are different this time. In the Internet bubble of the late 1990s, e-businesses with no revenues, let alone profits, were valued in the billions of dollars. "Eyeballs," a popular measurement of the number of people visiting e-commerce Web pages, were used to quantify and justify these valuations. Investors ignored traditional business realities, perhaps because they feared missing out on the "easy" money to be made. Today, eyeballs have been supplanted by more normal revenue-driven metrics, such as click-throughs to purchase.

In bubbles, valuations get so rich and offer so much promise of continuing to rise that transactions tend to involve more stock than cash. (Using one overheated currency to pay for another sometimes creates a natural hedge against the bubble. In 2001, AOL shareholders escaped the overheated Internet bubble by exchanging their stock for Time Warner's harder "old-world" currency.) Governance also gets sloppy during bubbles. Fearing any delay, executives commit to deals faster, without adequate due diligence and without determining how the deal fits into their long-term strategy; boards of directors tend to become more deferential to management.

In M&A, ultimately something rational—something quantifiable and credible—must underpin the drive to industry consolidation and price increases on acquisitions. For instance, when second-tier assets are selling at or above first-tier prices, buyers should explicitly ask whether they are in a bubble or a wave. During the late 1990s, it should have given buyers pause when the valuation of a newly founded e-company with millions in losses far exceeded that of a profitable, long-established brick-and-mortar company. Note that this is not an admonition against all "big bets." Some turn out to be very successful. In the 1980s and 1990s, the major agricultural chemicals firms engaged in bidding wars for the scarce delivery assets they needed to realize a long-term return from their biotechnology investments; they believed correctly that genetic technology alone would not be sufficient.

Another sign of bubbles is evidence of herd behavior. Yale economist Robert J. Shiller pegs "social contagion" as the most important element in detecting a speculative bubble. Recognizing social contagion, he says, "is a lot like understanding a disease epidemic." Like a disease epidemic, bubbles have a contagion rate (the rate at which people participate in the activity that supports the bubble) and a removal rate (the rate at which they abandon that behavior). "Sooner or later," says Shiller, who identified both the Internet bubble and the U.S. housing bubble in advance and forecast their implosions, "some factor boosts the infection rate sufficiently above the removal rate for an optimistic view of the market to become widespread. There is an escalation in public knowledge of the arguments that would seem to support that view, and soon the epidemic spirals out of control." Many cycles exhibit this pattern: first there is a legitimate change, then strategic buyers become active, then derivative strategic buyers and financially driven speculators join in, and finally the wave transforms into a full-fledged bubble.

In M&A bubbles, executives are driven to make deals for fear of missing out on near-term profits or long-term position. They may pursue mergers and acquisitions simply to block competitors, instead of being guided by their own strategic plan. Or they begin to pursue acquisitions in "hot" sectors in which they have little or no expertise. Wachovia's $25 billion acquisition of Golden West Financial in 2006 is an example of such a deal. Wachovia made the purchase to gain access to southern California's exotic ad-justable-rate mortgage market, one of the hottest real estate markets during the housing bubble and one of the hardest hit when that bubble burst a year later. Loans such as "pick a pay" mortgages, which allow borrowers to choose how much they want to repay, tacking any unpaid interest onto the loan amount, soon started to default at much higher than normal rates. By early 2008, Wachovia was forced to raise $7 billion in additional capital; in September 2008, the FDIC seized the banking giant, which was eventually acquired by Wells Fargo.

Before making any acquisition in a rising market, it behooves executives and boards to determine whether they're dealing with a bubble. For instance, in early 2008, speculation grew that the run-up in demand and prices for alternative energy, such as biofuels, was creating an M&A bubble in that sector. (A report at the time by Booz & Company and the World Economic Forum identified biofuel valuations as one possible emerging bubble.) An executive mulling an acquisition in that space at that particular point in history would have been wise to ask a series of questions, such as: Why didn't alternative energy take off during previous energy crises in the United States? Has technology progressed far enough to make alternative energy viable? Has the scientific evidence for global climate change—and in particular the link between biofuels and carbon emissions—become more compelling? Do government subsidies put the cost of alternative energies on a par with that of traditional energy?

Most important, would the economics of alternative energy work if the price of oil dropped below $100 per barrel? If so, is oil experiencing a bubble of its own—driven by speculators and panicky investors? Or has oil permanently reset at a higher price because of emerging market demand, thus creating an intrinsic change in the alternative energy sector that would solidly underpin a wave?

As it turned out, the answers to the last three questions could have been critical to a successful deal: in January 2009, oil was selling below $50 per barrel, the short-term economic case for alternative energy was much less compelling, and the valuations of alternative energy companies were far lower than they had been just months earlier. By the time this book appears, prices may have recalibrated again—at a higher or a lower level.

Complicating the calculus of deal making still further is the fact that even during a bubble, it may still make sense to proceed with an acquisition. A company may find itself at an ill-timed crossroads where, bubble or not, the strategic plan requires that the deal go forward. For instance, if a company needs to fill a critical link in its supply chain to lower costs across the entire enterprise, then any delay might be a strategically poor choice. As long as the deal is motivated by a long-term strategic plan and justified by proven valuations instead of "invented metrics," it's OK to buy during a bubble. But the buyer's deal strategy and deal-making skills must be especially sharp to meet the challenge.

TURNING BUBBLES AND WAVES INTO OPPORTUNITIES

The behavior of capital markets and acquiring firms provides a set of early signals to help executives decide whether

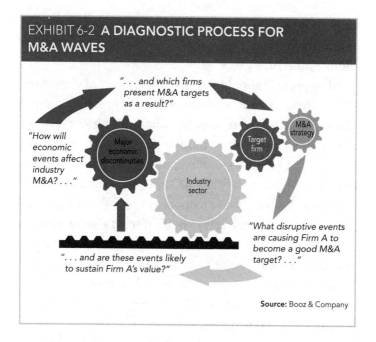

EXHIBIT 6-2 **A DIAGNOSTIC PROCESS FOR M&A WAVES**

". . . and which firms present M&A targets as a result?"

"How will economic events affect industry M&A? . . ."

Major economic discontinuities

Industry sector

Target firm

M&A strategy

"What disruptive events are causing Firm A to become a good M&A target? . . ."

". . . and are these events likely to sustain Firm A's value?"

Source: Booz & Company

an M&A environment resembles a wave, an inflating bubble, or a looming bust. In addition to a keen eye, an analytical skill set and a deft touch are also needed to translate observations of exploitable sector discontinuities into a profitable M&A strategy.

This suggests a disciplined, process-based approach to managing M&A during a wave, as illustrated by Exhibit 6-2. Each "gear" in the process represents a different analysis; together they add up to a deep understanding of the conditions that are creating the current environment. And they can be used to lay the groundwork for detailed sector and target firm views.

Each step in this diagnostic process adds another component necessary to creating a merganic strategy (as described in Chapter 7): a strategy synthesizing mergers and acquisitions, organic growth, and alliances into one co-herent game plan. That type of strategy can help you avoid bubbles and ride waves.

The process should start by taking a macro view of the discontinuities and conditions that are creating current market realities. Next comes an analysis of how these re-alities affect the relevant industry sectors. If this analysis reveals that M&A is a viable approach to growth for this company and industry at this time, the next step in the process is to identify target opportunities: deciding which individual firms are likely to benefit from a merger or ac-quisition, based on such factors as market share, costs, and revenues. Finally, with the most desirable targets identi-fied, a deal strategy is formulated and executed.

The goal of this process is to analyze whether the tar-get company is positioned to benefit relative to its peers. If the answers are positive, an acquisition is likely to be sound. If they aren't, the target's valuation and attractive-ness, which may be hard to resist, are probably less com-pelling than they seem because a bubble is at play.

This type of analysis is just the starting point. Bubbles and waves will be with us indefinitely; indeed, they will probably continue to occur more frequently and with greater amplitude than before. This is the future of M&A, and decision makers must prepare themselves for it. Though the challenges will be great, so will be the poten-tial rewards. Those companies that become skilled at managing bubbles and waves stand to meaningfully out-perform their rivals. Chapter 7 will show how a merganic strategy can help.

7

MERGANIC STRATEGY FOR A HYPERACTIVE ERA

THE DRIVE for scale. The ever-increasing velocity of capital and information, and the impatience that it spawns. Deep-pocketed competition everywhere. Whipsaw periods of consolidation driven by a confusing stream of bubbles, waves, and bubbles on top of waves. And increasingly volatile global economic cycles. These trends and conditions have produced a highly uncertain business atmosphere in the short term and a challenging, hyperactive growth environment that will probably continue well into the 2010s. It will offer numerous M&A opportunities, some leading to higher ground and some leading to quicksand.

Despite all of these dynamics, succeeding in such an environment will still require profitable growth at a rate that exceeds the industry average in up cycles and overcomes the macroeconomic constraints in down cycles. But how can a company count on growing at such a rate?

The merganic approach is based on the observation that sustained growth is the result of the continuous acquisition of new capabilities, not the pursuit of transient market positions. There are only three ways to develop the capabilities necessary for profitable growth. Companies can *make* capabilities, developing them organically by building on their existing businesses. They can *buy* capabilities, purchasing them through M&A and combining them with their own existing assets and prowess to boost the top line. Or they can *borrow* capabilities, pursuing them through virtual scale by using alliances and partnerships.

Successful companies, as we observed in Chapter 1, do not choose among making, buying, and borrowing capabilities. They conduct all three activities using a coordinated road map, with the same people involved in planning all three, so that the activities are mutually reinforcing. This is the core of a *merganic* approach to growth.

THE GROWTH TRINITY

No single type of growth can drive above-average performance over the long term or buck the macroeconomic cycle when it turns down. The three routes to growth are interdependent and need to be considered together if they are to reinforce one another and buttress the firm's overarching business theme.

To understand why this is so, consider each type of growth as a stand-alone approach. A company that relies solely on M&A for growth will tend to lose balance and bargaining power. When such companies seek complex acquisitions, beyond simple consolidations with other companies like themselves, they are more likely to define desirable targets in isolation from their overall growth strategies rather than in a holistic manner. Furthermore, their eagerness to make deals, if only because they see M&A as the single easy path to growth, will inevitably lead the company to overpay for some marginal properties. When making deals is the sole focus of an expansion strategy (as with roll-ups), companies often do not, or cannot, take the time to integrate and build upon their acquisitions or develop internal capabilities; the next deal will soon be on its way. The result is a trail of just barely knit together operations, neglected internal capabilities, and subpar organic growth. Finally, the investment community views such deals as a sign of poor strategy and frequently undervalues the transaction.

One might argue that if acquisitions are small, the repercussions of an ill-conceived or hurried execution are minimal. But there's a catch in practice: most deals can't be small when M&A is the sole source of growth. Rapid profitable growth is required, and if deals are the only vehicle for this, then some of them must be relatively large transactions that are capable of having a significant impact. This, in turn, greatly increases their complexity and worsens the odds of their success.

Citigroup followed a primarily deal-driven growth model from the late 1980s to the early 1990s, undertaking a decade-long blitzkrieg of acquisitions. It started in 1986 when Sanford "Sandy" Weill took private a company called Commercial Credit, a subsidiary of Control Data Systems.

Two years later, Commercial Credit acquired Primerica, a conglomerate that had already bought both life insurer A.L. Williams and stockbroker Smith Barney. Then, in September 1992, Primerica formed a strategic alliance with Travelers Insurance, which had suffered because of poor real estate investments and significant losses in the aftermath of Hurricane Andrew. A year later, the two merged, and the group became Travelers, Inc. During this period, Travelers acquired Shearson Lehman and merged it with Smith Barney. Then, in November 1997, Travelers Group (which had been renamed again in April 1995 when it merged with Aetna Property and Casualty, Inc.) made a $9 billion deal to purchase Salomon Brothers, a major bond trader and investment bank. The culmination of this rapid growth occurred on April 6, 1998, when the merger between Citicorp and Travelers Group was announced, creating a company with assets of almost $700 billion.

A decade later, the leaders of Citigroup were still trying to fully rationalize the bank's sprawling empire. In 2003 and 2005, retrenching began, and parts of the Travelers Insurance business were spun off and sold. Then-CEO Chuck Prince was quoted as saying, "The day of the transformative deal is over." The next CEO, Vikram Pandit, continued to divest businesses, including an Italian outsourcing franchise and German retail banking, even as the credit crisis of 2007 and 2008 added pressure. By 2008, more than 50,000 positions had been eliminated, and additional divestitures and headcount reductions had been announced. In January 2009, after drawing $45 billion in government loans, Citigroup posted a fourth-quarter loss of $8.29 billion—its fifth consecutive quarterly loss—and Pandit announced that he would split the company up, effectively dismantling Sandy Weill's financial supermarket.

To be sure, many financial firms were caught in the global credit crisis. But Citigroup was supposed to be different: it had been organized around the idea that M&A would provide the size, diversity, and coordination needed to insulate the company from the froth of economic upheaval. Instead, a too-wide strategic focus and an inability to efficiently transform deals into organic growth left it highly vulnerable in a crisis environment. This is a common long-term predicament for companies that rely solely upon mergers and acquisitions for growth.

But organic growth alone is no panacea either. Like M&A, organic growth—through the introduction of new products, expansion within current markets, or direct entry into new markets—by itself is not sufficient over the long term. There are two main reasons for this: the maturation of industries and the relativity of growth.

When an industry first emerges or when it undergoes a major shift that fundamentally expands its markets, high levels of organic growth are possible. For instance, where an expanding market is driving growth and a company can out-innovate or out-market its competition, other forms of growth may not be necessary at all. But sooner or later, these windows of opportunity will close. These days, the velocity trend is causing them to close faster than ever, as more and more competitors converge on the same set of opportunities, and the leaders' time-to-market advantages erode. Even in some new markets and new technologies, the rising complexity of offerings, or the rapid response of competitors, is driving companies to undertake M&A rather than attempt to go it alone. Monsanto and DuPont, for example, acquired seed and other companies during the 1990s to capture the full value of their innovations in agricultural biotechnology and to provide some defensibility against imitators. Moreover, as industries mature, it becomes harder and harder for companies to maintain a substantial edge, and their performance trends back to the median, which is not enough to satisfy the demand for superior performance. In short, organic growth tends to run out of gas as industries mature. At this point, well-conceived and well-executed mergers and acquisitions become necessary, along with the willingness to tap the virtual scale of alliances.

The second reason why organic growth alone tends not to be sustainable derives from William Barnett's Red Queen principle (noted in Chapter 1). A company's performance is meaningful only relative to that of its competitors; performance is not absolute. A company can have a high organic growth rate, but still fall behind relative to its industry, especially when its competitors pursue growth through M&A and alliances. The relative performance rates of companies are manifest in stock market valuations. This is why investment markets often factor in expectations of returns that for most industries would not be reasonable from organic growth alone. When this happens, the company must look beyond organic growth to acquisitions or alliances because staying the course of organic growth is tantamount to falling behind.

The third growth strategy, virtual scale, might seem at first blush to be an ideal compromise. It provides growth potential at much less expense than either going it alone or premium-laden acquisitions. By combining their assets and complementing one another's capabilities, companies can expand their operations faster and maintain more flexibility than with an outright purchase. As we saw in Chapter 1, joint ventures and the other forms of collaborative deals that provide virtual scale can enhance the clout of all the companies involved.

But in reality, as with M&A and organic growth, pursuing virtual scale as a dedicated growth strategy is untenable. Although alliances and partnerships certainly have their place, any experienced executive knows that they are often difficult to negotiate, manage, and sustain as the parent companies' motivations evolve. Multiplying the work involved in one such agreement by the number of alliances required to create sustained growth in a large company would result in a highly complex web of relationships. It also requires that revenues be split among the principals.

Furthermore, to be a desirable partner, a company must be able to contribute either tangible assets and capabilities or an entrée to markets and infrastructure. That means real-world know-how and hard assets—which can be built only through organic growth or acquisitions. The credit card giant VISA, Inc., now a public company, was founded as a vehicle for virtual scale, a cooperative that eventually included more than 21,000 banks and enabled each of them to extend payment and credit services to their customers across a global processing network. This virtual scale relationship was mutually beneficial and spurred tremendous growth in many banks. But it did not, by any stretch, excuse any of the banks from developing their core capabilities further, or from growing through appropriate acquisitions.

Finally, if a company were to lose its ability to pursue other means of growth, it would become dependent on its alliances; it would devolve to a subordinate role, akin to that of a captive supplier or customer. It would no longer be a true partner, and before long, most likely, either it would have to give up some of its margins and profits to the other partners, or it would be replaced.

BUILDING THE MERGANIC ROAD MAP: CAPABILITY CHAINING

A merganic approach to growth overcomes the limitations of M&A, organic growth, and virtual scale by combining them to create alternative paths to high performance. It is the basis for corporate expansion, diversification, and renewal. And *capability chaining* lies at the heart of a well-constructed merganic approach.

Capability chaining is the deliberate practice of sequencing corporate growth initiatives with an eye toward coherence, relative scale, and risk mitigation—building a portfolio of the skills, competencies, technologies, and processes that are integral parts of an overall business growth strategy.

"Capabilities are the particular ideas, skills and competencies that, when put together, enable a company to consistently attract its primary customers," wrote Cesare Mainardi, Paul Leinwand, and Steffen Lauster of Booz & Company in a 2008 article on this subject. "A portfolio of capabilities might include intellectual capital—patents, trademarks, products, and distinctive practices—but those elements are not enough. Patents expire. Premium products become commoditized. However, a distinctive combination of skills, tools, or processes, deployed in day-to-day business, will tend to get better over time, at a pace that prevents competitors from catching up."

Many companies start out at a disadvantage because they do not consider the three growth paths in a unified way when they plan and execute their growth strategies. Often, this happens because different functions and operating units within the firm focus on different means of achieving growth. The corporate or business development and finance departments typically want to buy growth, whereas the business units, the R&D and innovation teams, and the marketing and sales teams typically want to make growth. Alliances, meanwhile, tend to receive little support in many companies. And all too often, the separation of these teams from one another leads to a disconnected approach to growth rather than a tightly woven tapestry.

One symptom of this is miscommunication; another symptom is difficulty reconciling alternative investment options. Different parts of the firm can work at cross-purposes because each group is not sufficiently aware of what the others are doing. Moreover, potential avenues of growth can be missed because some of the teams are unfamiliar with them. R&D departments may ignore licensing or alliances or treat them as a last resort, to be pursued only after internal efforts at innovation and renewal fall short. This occurs despite the well-documented success of external innovation programs, such as Procter & Gamble's "Connect + Develop" initiative. Connect + Develop involves external R&D partnerships with a variety of groups (including some competitors) and has led to many successful products. Further evidence of the value of R&D

alliances comes from a Booz & Company study of pharmaceutical companies that identified windows in time when the values of in-licensed compounds were higher than those of in-house initiatives.

An examination of companies with records of long-term growth, such as General Electric Company and The Walt Disney Company, shows that the development or acquisition of new capabilities was instrumental in their success. General Electric, for instance, was founded by Thomas Edison in 1890, and only a few years later began producing electric cooking devices. But the most effective cookstove designs belonged to two other early-twentieth-century companies, Hughes (founded by George Hughes, the inventor of the electric cooking range) and Hotpoint, based in St. Louis. In 1918, GE acquired both of those companies in a merger of their appliance businesses. All through the 1920s and 1930s, GE expanded its technical capabilities and its product lines through innovation and alliances, until there were a variety of GE laundry and kitchen machine factories around the United States.

Then in 1953, responding to the emerging consumer market for major appliances in the United States, the company moved most of these operations to a new 700-acre "appliance park" factory in Louisville, Kentucky. Having its entire business colocated in one spot gave GE a way to develop and deploy capabilities across a wide range of machines. For example, in 1955, GE's newfound ability to create designer-colored coatings allowed consumers to order matching refrigerators, dishwashers, and stoves in pink, yellow, or turquoise. As the company evolved, its capabilities evolved as well. These included technological R&D in the 1960s (when GE introduced the self-cleaning oven);

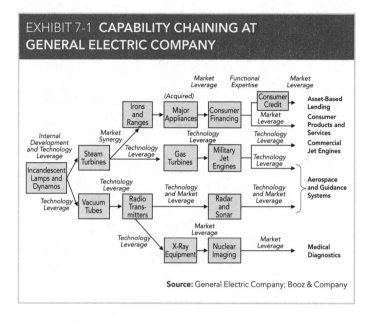

EXHIBIT 7-1 **CAPABILITY CHAINING AT GENERAL ELECTRIC COMPANY**

Source: General Electric Company; Booz & Company

revitalized marketing in the 1970s; a joint venture with GE Credit Corporation in the 1980s, to help customers afford major appliances, that ultimately became a key component of the growth of GE Financial Services; and an in-depth quality improvement program, linked to Six Sigma, in the 1990s. As seen in Exhibit 7-1, the appliances case represented one of many similar GE moves, enabled by the organizational capabilities of the previous round and the rewards inherent in those capabilities. In addition to taking full advantage of capability-based expansion, GE's example illustrates the use of a full array of available capabilities—technology and market-based—as opposed to getting railroaded onto one growth track.

The same underlying pattern of capability linking can be seen at Disney. Disney's original business of making short animated films led to its pioneering and highly

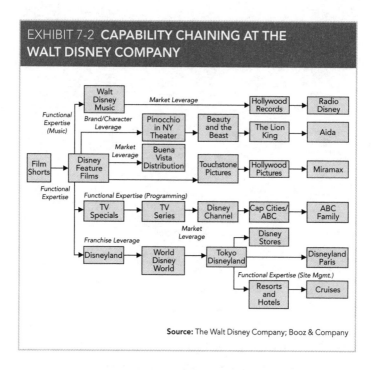

EXHIBIT 7-2 **CAPABILITY CHAINING AT THE WALT DISNEY COMPANY**

Source: The Walt Disney Company; Booz & Company

popular animated feature films. This, in turn, gave the company the expertise to develop its own distinctive line of live-action features. These provided the financial and brand leverage to launch the Disneyland theme park. The films also gave the company the functional expertise in music to allow it to create Walt Disney Music and then Hollywood Records. Disney Feature Films also led to the functional expertise in programming to create TV specials and eventually to the Disney-ABC television franchise. As shown in Exhibit 7-2, step by step, capability by capability, Disney branched into a variety of other businesses: toys, resorts, cruises, product licensing, retail, and theater. The common thread through all these diverse businesses is a sensibility and a basic target audience that allow both customers and employees to easily recognize when something fits the Disney brand and when it does not.

A capability-chaining approach has a few basic components: a theme that will guide the construction of each chain, a starting point grounded in existing or readily accessible capabilities, and an approach for identifying opportunities to develop desired capabilities that enables companies to see beyond their current situations. This last component is critical: a company that persists in staying close to its core skills may be fortunate enough to be in a segment with high naturally occurring growth, or it may be more akin to a person who has topped out in his career, unable to stretch beyond his current skills and level. A capability-chain-based strategy involves deliberately planning long-term "stretch" journeys (or at least journeys that are intended to last beyond a few quarters) such as those that GE, Disney, and other successful companies have made. Sophisticated executives have learned to look strategically at their capabilities: to examine how the enterprise is organized, how systems and practices fit together, and how all these factors can be arranged and enhanced to separate a company from its competitors. Capability chaining is a proven planning tool and has been used successfully by Booz & Company for several decades. But its focus in this book is its usefulness in helping to navigate the five trends outlined earlier.

Once a company identifies the capabilities that are needed in order to begin or continue along a leg of its journey, it faces a set of critical decisions about how it will obtain, develop, and master these capabilities. The most basic of these decisions revolve around the question of whether to make, buy, or borrow the many skills and assets that compose an organizational capability. The merganic approach examines each make versus buy versus borrow decision as part of an integrated whole.

A capability-driven merganic approach judges each new acquisition, alliance, or organic growth opportunity on the basis of how well it will further the company's important capabilities. For example, UnitedHealthcare, one of the largest health insurers in the United States, has acquired the consumer-driven health plan specialist Definity Health, the insurer Golden Rule, and the IT solutions provider Claredi, and it has set up partnerships with MasterCard, Discover Card, and the credit card processor TSYS. These deals are best understood from a capabilities perspective. In the United States, health savings accounts (HSAs) have emerged as a financial vehicle that allows people to accumulate assets to fund future medical expenses. With claims-processing capabilities as the starting point, the emergence of consumer health-related financial products (such as HSAs) as a catalyst, and U.S. companies reducing their contributions to health costs (especially for retirees) as the environmental context, a health insurance company would need to access new capabilities for financial planning and investment to become a leader in any future health/wealth services market. United Healthcare appears to be using a merganic approach in positioning itself around this theme.

Every time a new business is launched along the chain or an old business is repositioned there, corporate leaders must focus on gaining the additional capabilities (beyond those needed for entry) that are required to succeed in that business. After entry into a new market in Latin America, for example, they may decide that they need expert marketing skills for that region, or that they need to develop a Pacific Rim manufacturing and supply chain footprint. They then decide whether to develop those capabilities internally (make 'em), obtain them from an alliance partner (borrow 'em), or seek an M&A deal with a company that has them (buy 'em). This merganic approach supports management as it grows the company's capability chain link by link, business by business.

MERGANIC BENEFITS AND THE FIVE TRENDS

A merganic road map to growth ensures that everyone in the company is on the same page and that the trade-offs between making, buying, or borrowing are clear. The merganic road map offers additional benefits that lead directly to more successful mergers and acquisitions, as shown in Exhibit 7-3.

First, this approach ensures that deals are not pursued for their own sake or for the wrong reasons, and that growth initiatives will be relatively coherent. Coherence is essential, as companies increasingly will be driven to compete on the basis of relevant scale, the first trend that is influencing M&A activity in the current environment. Coherence enables companies to avoid the conglomerate trap—a rather blunt instrument in which high-growth targets are pursued for their market positions and financial synergies, with scant regard for how closely the acquisition's capabilities mesh with the acquirer's. The conglomerate model persists all too often, despite its high price tag and the fact that most executives intellectually understand

EXHIBIT 7-3 A MERGANIC APPROACH TO THE FIVE TRENDS

Trend	Challenges to Strategic Buyers	Merganic Benefits
Size	Building relevant scale and coherence	• Well–defined, capability-based themes (vs. vague "umbrellas") • Tangible linkages to value (i.e., economic or customer acquisition advantages)
Velocity and Impatience	Moving with deliberate speed	• Constant readiness (i.e., ever-green map of opportunities and acquisition/alliance candidates) • Shared context for quickly assessing and communicating new deal options • Touchstone to simultaneously coordinate logic for multiple deal opportunities • Pre-agreed communications vehicle ("why we are doing this")
New Blues	Understanding New Blues' expansion strategies	• Road map for long-term investment (vs. responses to short-term fluctuations) • Tool for evaluating competitor motivations and next moves
	Competing with new strategic buyers for traditional Blue Chips	• Buy vs. alliance option analysis • Tool for evaluating competitor motivations and next moves • Differentiated "puzzle piece" value
Financial Buyers	Competing with agile, deep-pocketed non-traditional buyers	• Ability to analyze deals and prepare offers based on multiple value dimensions (i.e., strategic "puzzle piece" value vs. stand-alone value)
Waves and Bubbles	Managing through uncertainty	• Ability to calculate deal value, independent of the external froth • Method for identifying the existence and value of alternative targets

the value of coherence. Often, the best evidence of coherence is the sequence of merganic events: GE developed a successful nuclear imaging business on the foundation laid by its x-ray business. Similarly, Disney used the capabilities developed in its theme parks to establish its own uniquely targeted cruise line.

The second benefit of a merganic approach to growth is the benefit of choice and the flexibility that choice engenders. As the famous quote (originally by American psychologist Abraham Maslow) put it, "It is tempting, if the only tool you have is a hammer, to treat everything as if it were a nail." In the same vein, when a business unit or function believes that it has only one route to growth—whether that route be organic or alliance or acquisition—its options, and thus its potential, are reduced. Merganic road maps require expansive thinking about the definition of a capability, helping chemical companies think beyond molecular science, for example, and consumer companies reach beyond brand for sources of advantage. In turn, such thinking opens up new M&A alternatives and provides nonstandard responses to traditional and nontraditional competition.

Because a merganic approach provides a full growth toolkit, a company can decide which means of growth makes the most sense in a given situation. This is particularly valuable during a recession or a time of economic turbulence, when the opportunities for organic growth are limited because of the constriction of existing markets and profit margins. Stronger companies that approach growth in a merganic way are likely to find that the reduced valuations of other companies make acquisitions more attractive. Merganically oriented companies that can't afford to buy growth are likely to turn to alliances and partnerships.

The third benefit of a merganic approach is the constant state of readiness that it produces, which enables deal makers to manage the velocity that is affecting every aspect of business. When corporate leaders know their road maps, potential and even unforeseen acquisition candidates can be assessed rapidly for strategic fit, and synergy conversations with boards and due diligence teams can be grounded quickly in substantive linkages and advantages. These executives become faster and more nimble; they are always scanning the horizon for opportunities, ready to outmaneuver rivals through acquisitions, organic growth, or virtual scale. In this perpetual state of readiness, a company is always reassessing its strategy, capabilities, and possible targets, and can react more quickly when an opportunity arises.

Klaus Kühn, the chief financial officer of the German chemical and pharmaceuticals giant Bayer AG, recently recalled how his company's continual state of alertness facilitated its celebrated acquisition of Schering in 2006. "That was our biggest transaction so far, but also one of our quickest in execution. . . . From the time that [Bayer's rival Merck KAaG] announced its bid, we had just 11 days to come up with a counterbid and a full financing package," said Kühn. "[But] we had already done our homework well before the Merck offer. Because we wanted to expand our health-care business, we had started looking for potential targets specifically in pharmaceuticals and OTC, the over-the-counter business. . . . When the Schering opportunity came up, we didn't have to do any deep analysis. It was already on our list."

This heightened state of readiness is an important mechanism for coping with bubbles. Whenever markets get frothy, fast action and sound judgment are required. A merganic approach is a rudder that deal makers can use to steer safely toward their strategic goals. It also ensures that deal makers understand the big picture, which provides both a sanity test for valuations and a competitive advantage as more competitors with deeper pockets, such as the New Blues and financial buyers, enter the game.

WINNING WITH A MERGANIC APPROACH

A few companies have already captured the benefits of a merganic approach to growth. Danaher, the $19 billion diversified industrial company introduced in Chapter 1, is one. This company employs a mix of M&A, organic growth, and virtual scale to beat market indexes by a wide margin.

Danaher complements its long-standing track record of organic growth (4 to 6 percent compound annual growth rate) with alliances, such as the partnership between Danaher subsidiary Leica Microsystems and Veeco Instruments, and an active portfolio approach that balances divestitures, "bolt-on" acquisitions that expand current businesses and capabilities, and "new platform" acquisitions that establish new businesses and capabilities.

Another company that has taken a merganic approach to growth is News Corporation, the global media giant created by Rupert Murdoch. Murdoch has repeatedly confounded critics and experts and has navigated successfully through an industry that has faced shrinking revenues and profits for the last few decades.

News Corp.'s Fox Network in the United States is an especially interesting case. Its roots go back to Murdoch's 1985 purchase of TCF Holdings, the parent of the 20th Century Fox movie studio. Murdoch quickly followed up this deal, which brought News Corp. a film production and distribution capability, with a $1.5 billion purchase of six local television stations in the United States. Then he boldly announced his plan to create the Fox Broadcasting Network, a fourth television network in a country in which three networks—ABC, NBC, and CBS—had dominated the industry for decades.

The success of the Fox Network was built on a merganic combination of innovation, acquisition, and alliances. 20th Century Fox began producing innovative programming for the new television network. Programs such as *Married . . . with Children* and *The Simpsons* changed the face of prime-time programming. The network successfully allied itself with the National Football League, paying almost $1.6 billion for a four-year contract to air *Monday Night Football*. With that lucrative franchise in hand, Fox purchased stakes in more television stations. With one capability-based expansion after another, News Corp. successfully created a new network in U.S. broadcast television.

This process of building the audience and the station affiliate network through the merganic development of new programming, alliances, and acquisitions has continued ever since. In the process, Fox's performance has outstripped that of its competitors. CNNMoney.com editor at large Paul la Monica reports in his recent book, *Inside Rupert's Brain*, "In February 2004, Fox won its first so-called sweeps month, a key period used by networks and marketers to establish advertising rates for the upcoming season. The network went on to win the ratings battle for the 18-49-year-old demographic for the entire 2004-2005 season and did so again the next two seasons. Fox also won the ratings race in 2007-2008. In fact, through early March 2008, Fox was the only network to see a boost in viewers for the 2007-2008 television season."

When fully developed, a merganic approach to growth becomes a capability in and of itself. Where, then, does a corporate leader begin in developing the capability of sustained merganic growth? Most companies need to improve all three core practices—mergers and acquisitions, organic growth, and alliances. But few companies recognize the value of tying all three together via an approach to growth strategy that is visionary, yet grounded in step-by-step logic. By rigorously coordinating a company's deal making, alliances, and organic growth efforts into one overarching effort, corporate leaders can focus their collective mindset on continuous long-term growth.

We do not cover organic growth and alliances in depth in this book because they are outside its scope—and because the nature of these practices depends, in part, on your company's specific industry and situation. But the development of better merger and acquisition practices applies to all industries, and it can provide a basis for developing other capabilities later. The best practices for mergers and acquisitions, and their evolution among well-managed companies in the future, is the topic of the next and final chapter.

8

CRAFTING THE SUCCESSFUL DEAL

NOT LONG AGO, when the pace of business was slower, a company might have had a chance to recover if its M&A initiatives faltered. Today, as many corporate leaders are undertaking deals of greater complexity and broader range than they would have contemplated a few years ago, the margin for error is much reduced.

Together, the five trends described in this book have created an environment in which the skills of deal making matter tremendously—and cannot be taken for granted. The rise in the size and scale of deals, the velocity of business transactions and information, the impatience of capital, the emergence of new global "blue chip" companies, the encroachment by financial buyers, and the increasing number of bubbles and waves have all raised the stakes on successful mergers and acquisitions. These changes have made it more difficult for companies to forgo acquisitions,

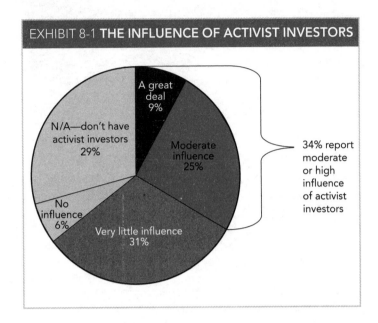

EXHIBIT 8-1 THE INFLUENCE OF ACTIVIST INVESTORS

A great deal 9%

N/A—don't have activist investors 29%

Moderate influence 25%

No influence 6%

Very little influence 31%

34% report moderate or high influence of activist investors

and more difficult for companies to recover after deals that do not go well.

Activist stakeholders, including but not limited to powerful financial buyers, have also helped shape this new, less forgiving context. Activist investors (especially institutions holding large blocks) are gaining board-level influence, are paying more attention to the use of mergers and acquisitions in corporate strategy, and are more demanding judges of performance. The result, as shown in Exhibit 8-1, is more and more CEOs being held responsible for underperformance.

These pressures were exacerbated by the collapse of the credit bubble in 2008 and the ensuing downturn in the global economy. Investors were caught off guard by the speed and scale of wealth destruction. For many, this is the third time in a decade that they have been surprised by a rapid fall to earth—the collapse of the dot-com bubble, "convergence-based" deals, and high-leverage acquisitions—and they are now less likely to accept at face value any company's stated rationale for a deal. In the new environment, capital is more expensive, the time granted to produce results is shorter, and there is less slack in the balance sheet to recover from missteps. The company that stumbles in its M&A conception and execution is even more likely to be besieged from all sides. Analysts grow skeptical, investors look for the exits, employees get restless, regulators and prosecutors may get curious, and competitors pounce. Hence the need for improved deal-making capabilities.

Chapter 7 described how a merganic approach, including a detailed capabilities-based road map, provides a strategic context for growth, identifying whether to buy (versus make or borrow), what to buy, and from whom to buy. This chapter is focused on the "hows" of deal making in this still-emerging environment. It describes how to build a sound predeal business case, how deal evaluation needs to evolve, and how to plan and execute a successful integration. Our purpose is to offer some observations and insights into ways in which the most sophisticated companies are advancing the art and science of M&A planning and execution in light of the five trends discussed earlier. The precepts in this chapter are intended to be both descriptive (identifying what good companies are doing) and prescriptive (laying out a path for companies that want to thrive merganically). World-class M&A capabilities are not built overnight; they are developed and refined in an ongoing journey over several years and multiple transactions. In this chapter, we hope to provide a glimpse of the insights, skills, and methods that a company's leaders can pick up along the way.

AN OVERLAPPING FOUR-STAGE APPROACH

The process of designing, negotiating, and executing any individual M&A deal has four distinct stages. First, the predeal business case must be developed, validated, and approved. In the past, the business case was mainly financial in nature, with a high-level strategy overlay. In a world shaped by the five trends, the business case must include more and deeper strategic insight, as well as identify major planning and execution issues. Second is the deal-making stage, which traditionally includes the offer, negotiation, financing, and due diligence. In the new environment, due diligence carries a heavier load, paralleling the evolving business case requirements. Third is the design of a detailed integration plan for the combined organization. Finally, the deal must be executed successfully, smoothly, and with deliberate speed.

Many companies approach the overall deal process as if it were a linear process. They manage the four stages as if they were handing off the baton in a relay race: from the boardroom to the negotiating team to the integration planning program leaders to line management.

In a traditional world, a linear approach creates numerous obstacles to successful deals; in the new world, such an approach cannot adequately respond to the five trends and their implications. It lengthens the deal's timeline and exacerbates the impact of delays. This exposes the company to the impatience of the markets and gives competitors an opportunity to react. Impatience, along with the inefficiency of linear sequencing, adds to the pressure to complete each stage in less time; this, in turn, generally translates into less comprehensive understanding and planning. Issues that would be better addressed in an early stage of the deal process often surface in later stages. If the deal is executed sequentially, this can result in additional work, delays, and suboptimal solutions. Finally, a linear approach limits timely and open communication among the many teams and individuals involved in a deal. There is less opportunity for feedback—and the early warnings and robust solutions that it engenders—when information and decisions are simply passed from the team at one stage to the team at the next.

The solution is a more concurrent, holistic, "living" approach to the deal process—much like modern product development processes, where product design is informed concurrently by manufacturing requirements and marketing needs, rather than the old style "toss it over the fence" model. In a high-performance deal process, aspects of all four stages are pursued somewhat in parallel (with substantial overlap and continuous referencing back and forth) by a common team whose members are provided with mechanisms to help them communicate easily and regularly with each other and with the rest of the organization. For example, business case development includes downstream integration design awareness; due diligence findings are reexamined and revalidated later in integration planning. This type of process is simpler in terms of oversight but places greater demands on resources, time, and staff. However, as we show in the following sections, the results it produces are worth the added effort.

STAGE 1: BUILDING AN ENHANCED PREDEAL BUSINESS CASE

When a company is thinking about growth in merganic terms and has developed a capabilities-based road map, as described in Chapter 7, much of the groundwork that has traditionally been associated with creating a business case has already been completed. The merganic road map provides the strategic foundation for understanding the kinds of deals that a company should pursue and establishes a sanity check for the logic for each specific proposed deal. With a merganic road map in hand, the first stage of the deal process doesn't have to get bogged down in time-consuming "why this/why now" rationale creation. Instead, it can be more sharply focused on gathering information about a particular target, validating the assumptions about strategic fit, and building a deep understanding of the inherent and action elements of the deal—an understanding that illuminates the buyer's eventual freedom and constraints within the deal (see "Inherent and Action Elements," p. 164).

In this stage, the M&A team develops an objective assessment of the deal's value and likelihood of success. In an environment of skeptical stakeholders, a business case that features too broad a market assessment or too narrow a synergy analysis will not be acceptable. Instead, the old style "snapshot" view of the deal's near-term financial attractiveness—which typically included only a vague description of long-term benefits and little discussion of potential execution problems—will be replaced with a well-crafted business case featuring a more dynamic, comprehensive portrait of why a transaction makes sense today and over time.

The core of this process is a robust analysis showing whether or not the combined company can realize the full value of the transaction. The buyer examines the influence that the macro environment, including customers, suppliers, competitive dynamics, and the broader industry and economic environments, might have on the deal. This might mean answering questions such as "How well does our view of the target reflect the potential impact of changes in the business environment?" "What are we assuming about the regulatory environment?" "What are we assuming about customers?" "What are we assuming about pricing and the response of our competitors?" "And how might those assumptions, often developed from our first impressions, differ from reality?" The goal is to answer these questions based on future scenarios as well as the current situation, and for nontraditional competitors as well as traditional bidders.

The next business case issue that has risen in prominence is a pragmatic view of whether the combined company can succeed in the longer term. This entails asking questions to determine whether the merged firm will have the ability and capacity to make the acquisition successful, such as "What capabilities does the acquired company bring, and where are there capability gaps that could threaten the new company's success?" "Given the merger's constraints and commitments, can we successfully integrate the purchase?" "What will the talent attrition rate be, and in which functions—for example, operations, R&D, or sales?" "What integration challenges do we anticipate, and how will we handle them?" The answers to these questions provide the beginnings of a sound platform for the merger or acquisition because they require the creation of an initial hypothesis about how the purchased property will be integrated, and tee up questions for the due diligence and integration design stages.

The process includes an assessment of the attractiveness of the overall market and the competitive position of the target—and how these might change over time. In this quest, the team must gaze into the future and estimate the competitive position of the *combined* entity, including its impact on customers, competitors, and overall market dynamics. (For instance, will the merger invite new entrants into the market?) Bear in mind that the ways in which customers and competitors react to the merger can threaten value-creation assumptions.

INHERENT AND ACTION ELEMENTS

The leverage that buyers (or sellers) have in any deal, beyond the sum of money brought to the table, is dependent on two factors: those characteristics of a deal over which companies have little or no control (*inherent* elements) and those elements in which the actions you take during the deal process can substantially affect the outcome (*action* elements). Both types of elements are present in every deal, but companies that recognize the differences between the two and respond accordingly, significantly increase their chances of success.

Inherent Elements: Beyond Your Control

The captain of a boat, or the pilot of an airplane, pays close attention to the weather before departure. It may be out of her control, but what is happening and what could happen are critical to survival. She modifies her preparations, adjusts the planned routing, predetermines escape paths, and, most important of all, rethinks the go/no-go decision. In the same way, a skillful deal maker pays close attention to the inherent elements: those fixed or partly fixed qualities of the two companies that are being brought together.

Inherent elements are generally identifiable at the outset of a deal. They either can't be changed or would require a great deal of effort to change. They can include external characteristics, such as the regulatory and legal environment in which the buyer and the seller operate, the macroeconomic situation, and aspects of the five trends discussed in this book. (For example: Is the target company from an emerging market, and thus facing competition from New Blues? What stage of the economic cycle are we in? Are we riding a wave or buying into a bubble? Is this business in the public eye or politically sensitive?)

Inherent elements also include characteristics that exist in either the buyer's or the seller's businesses, such as their physical locations and footprints, their supply chain networks, their technologies, their shareholder profiles, and the leadership and culture within the companies. These inherent elements are often quasi-fixed characteristics; they may be within the deal maker's control after the deal closes, but they cannot be changed within the time frame of the negotiations.

A full accounting for the constraints created by an inherent element can make the difference between a viable deal and one that has no sustainable rationale. For example, if a buyer targets a company based in a country with strict labor laws, those laws need to be factored into the purchase decision. If these laws create major obstacles to the deal, perhaps blocking essential synergies that require headcount reduction or new work rules, the buyer may have little choice but to look elsewhere for a target.

The 2008 merger of the only two U.S.-based satellite radio companies, Sirius and XM, is a good example of a deal where exogenous constraints changed the value of the combination. In 1997, when the Federal Communications Commission (FCC) granted the companies their operating licenses, it had stipulated that to avoid a monopoly, they could never combine. Neither Sirius nor XM had any control over this inherent element, and, as it turned out, gaining approval for the merger deal consumed 18 months. During the approval delay, the world changed. The U.S. automobile industry—the primary source of new satellite radio customers—collapsed, other competitors grew stronger, the credit markets collapsed, the economy soured, the company's debt came due, and the financial structure of the combined company became untenable. In February 2009, months after the deal closed and the work of capturing synergies was well underway, the stock price of Sirius XM Radio had fallen to under 10 cents and the company narrowly avoided bankruptcy thanks to a cash infusion from Liberty Media.

Sirius XM is not alone. When Shell and Exxon-Mobil combined their lubricating oils chemical additives businesses in 1999, they did so knowing that the industry's standards-setting regime for motor oil performance would continue to constrain their options for innovation and value capture. When Bank of America combined with Merrill Lynch in 2009, it inherited an investment banking culture very different from traditional retail banking. Inherent elements can color every aspect of M&A, but they often can be managed when factored into valuation, integration challenges, and deal terms early in the deal-making process. If deal makers wait until later in the process, their options become fewer and the cost of responding to those characteristics can get much larger.

Action Elements: Subject to Design

The *action elements* of an acquisition are the factors influenced by the participants' own choices and decisions. Action elements might include the proper alignment of the deal with the corporate strategy, the transaction's terms, the creation of the business case and its communication to investors and other stakeholders, the quality of the negotiations, the interaction of the leadership teams of the companies involved in the merger, and, most important, the planning and execution of the integration.

Although action elements can make or break a merger or acquisition as easily as inherent elements can, deal makers have a much greater degree of control over them—at least in theory. In practice, getting the right outcomes is often much more difficult than many deal makers expect. When a merger looks good on paper and sports a compelling rationale, but never lives up to its promise, the cause of the problem can often be found in the action elements. For example, at least part of Citigroup's dilemma in the wake of the collapse of the credit bubble can be attributed to the difficulties it encountered in integrating the deals that it had made in the previous two decades and the resulting high costs and high headcount that burdened the company afterwards.

Companies often have significant latitude in managing the action elements of a deal. Also, smartly executed action elements can sometimes offset the impediments created by inherent elements. For instance, when pharmacy benefits manager Caremark Rx (now part of CVS Caremark) acquired its main competitor AdvancePCS, it adjusted its integration approach and designs to account for the fact that AdvancePCS served a large number of health insurers, whereas Caremark was oriented primarily toward direct employer-based services. This was an inherent difference with implications for IT integration, drug procurement policies, and transition planning.

This kind of preoffer work helps companies avoid M&A missteps before an offer is tendered. It creates the kind of clarity that includes knowing when it makes sense to pay more (for example, when a transaction, because of its fit in the broader road map, is worth more than its stand-alone value) and when to walk away from a deal. In the past, companies almost never pulled out of deals. Once initiated, deals seemed to take on a life of their own unless negotiations around price or senior management roles could not be resolved. Today, in an environment of velocity and impatience and waves and bubbles, successful deal makers carefully define and adhere to a broader set of triggers that could cause a transaction to become unattractive, and they demur if the warning signals are too daunting.

The enhanced business case also articulates a vision for where the acquisition may lead, including the potential for additional investments and opportunities that stretch beyond the stand-alone, short-term view. Today, stakeholders are more frequently asking, "What's next?" Stand-alone value is often insufficient when competing with financial buyers or New Blues with very different motivations and financing.

Stakeholders are also demanding that companies stand behind those rationales throughout the rest of the process. As noted in the Glaxo example, cited in Chapter 3, a well-crafted, long-term story is needed to augment short-term financial analyses. The enhanced business case, supported by a merganic road map that outlines what comes next, is particularly important for deals sold as growth plays. Finally, this stage provides a process for establishing the deal's valuation, its structure, and an approach strategy that raises the odds of a successful transaction.

Johnson & Johnson has proven itself adept at this stage of the deal process over the course of roughly 70 acquisitions since the late 1990s. In describing two deals—a $23 billion offer for Guidant, which J&J decided to abandon when the bidding rose too high, and a $16.6 billion deal for Pfizer's consumer health-care business, which was successfully concluded—CFO Dominic Caruso makes clear that the business cases in the two were quite different, but were equally well thought out.

"We always begin with our strategy," explains Caruso. "[The Guidant transaction was an] opportunity to add a microelectronics capability that was primarily implemented in our market approach to cardiac rhythm management. But the real underlying capability that existed there was the microelectronics. We went after it as an opportunity to add that new base of technology to the business.

"Pfizer represented a different kind of opportunity; they were strong in certain geographic markets where we weren't. For instance, we had a much stronger presence in China than Pfizer did. That was good because it meant we could sell more of their products there. Whereas in a market like Mexico, Pfizer had stronger ties than we did. So that turned out to be a nice set of complementary growth enablers. They were strong where we were weak and vice versa."

The overall tone of an enhanced business case is very different from the past. Its primary goal is to objectively test assumptions rather than, as in the past, build an argument for the deal. (In fact, in our recent work, we have been explicitly treating the business case and deal "packaging" as separate deliverables.) It seeks to identify questions and concerns early to better prepare the due diligence and integration design efforts. It probes inherent elements to identify where valuation adjustments or integration workarounds will be required. The enhanced business case provides more and deeper insights now, to offset the velocity and impatience that will inevitably arise during the due diligence, negotiation, and planning that follow later.

STAGE 2:
STRATEGIC DUE DILIGENCE

The second stage of the process has two traditional goals. First, the parties must agree on the deal's terms and conditions. Second, the deal must be verified and validated. Traditional due diligence represents a continuation of the testing and validation of the assumptions within the business case about the acquisition's value, including how the collaboration and combination created by the deal will yield incremental value. These two tasks—agreement negotiation and due diligence—are undertaken concurrently because the process of due diligence tests the proposed terms, and the results of these tests often require changes in the deal's terms.

A traditional due diligence exercise is limited by time but also by its narrow scope. It is defined and undertaken

EXHIBIT 8-2 THE EXPANDED INTENT OF MERGANIC DUE DILIGENCE		
Due Diligence Approach	**Components**	**Intent**
Traditional	Legal and Financial	➤ Are the risks acceptable? ➤ Is the price right?
Merganic	Strategic	➤ Will the deal succeed? • Are the business case assumptions valid? • Will the ability and capacity to execute exist? • What exogenous factors (regulatory, competitive, bubbles/cycles, etc.) could affect the outlook? • Which "what if" scenarios should be considered? • What integration issues require testing and deal design consideration?

to validate, verify, and "stress test" mainly the financial and legal aspects of the business case. But as business cases become more robust, as described in Stage 1, due diligence must also become more comprehensive and thorough than it was before, as seen in Exhibit 8-2.

While financial and legal due diligence validate the deal's near-term value, *strategic* due diligence adds another level of validation. In Stage 1, the enhanced business case attempted to be as objective as possible about an expanded list of questions; Stage 2 further verifies whether the business case for the deal—however enticing—is realistic. To test the assumptions in the business case, buyers need to push themselves to identify problems that might derail the deal down the road. Strategic due diligence seeks to answer two questions: First, is the combined company's value story viable? In other words, is it reasonable to conclude that the deal will produce an enduring, attractive economic return? Second, can we validate the business case finding that the participating companies have the skills necessary to deliver on that promise?

Strategic due diligence begins with the same types of questions as the enhanced business case: "How will potential competitors (including the nontraditional financial buyers and New Blues) view the deal, and how may they respond?" "Will the deal deliver the necessary short-term returns, and can it capture its intended long-term benefits?" "What about the out-years?" "Have we fully accounted for inherent limitations and for the effects of bubbles and waves?" "Are the targeted long-term benefits realistic, attainable, *and* sustainable?"

Strategic due diligence provides an additional layer of comfort that the deal value can be realized by the management team of the combined enterprise. One recent example of what that might entail is provided by a company that engaged a search firm to build an outside-in profile of all of the top talent in a target company, with the goal of understanding "whom we are getting and who is important to our business case" long before traditional postannouncement selection processes began. Beyond financial risks, there are material risks, such as technology issues and culture challenges, that must be identified and characterized even if solutions cannot be fully developed at this early stage. In addition to testing the business case, this expands the basis for the integration plan that will be crafted in the third stage. For example, if the due diligence team discovers that preserving the increased market share that the deal is supposed to deliver is a key driver of value, the combined company will need a proactive plan for fending off competitors who might try to pick off key customers.

In a recent interview, Chief Financial Officer Marcus Schenck of the German energy service provider E.ON described the company's strategic due diligence process like this: "Once our people have developed a business plan for a possible takeover target, we ask tough questions to see whether they really have thought everything through. 'Is there really a market? Are market price assumptions realistic? What do we know about the costs? Will there be regulatory hurdles? How easy will it be to implement this? What will be the competitive reaction?' . . . Of course you have to have a good grip on the financials, but you also have to have a gut feeling for the things that could go wrong and where to find them."

THE DUE DILIGENCE TEAM

The value of due diligence depends on the quality of the team that is in charge of the process. The right team brings the right skills and influence, which include the authority to kill the transaction if the business case and/or the anticipated synergies are unattainable. There are six guiding principles for boosting the effectiveness of a due diligence team:

1. Team members must represent all areas of the organization that will be affected by the transaction. This ensures that the right expertise is brought to bear early, and eases later acceptance by internal experts and management.

2. Since the due diligence process must be conducted on a very tight schedule, the team members should be relieved of other responsibilities and offered as many resources as possible: equipment, support staff, and access to data.

3. The senior leadership must communicate with the due diligence team so that the strategic and financial rationales behind the acquisition are clearly understood from the outset. Also, the team must be familiar with the details of the business case. That way, the team wastes no time as it tests assumptions, homes in on specific issues, and identifies the analysis and data required.

4. The due diligence team must master the art of gathering information in environments where confidentiality usually limits access to people and information. Too often, teams are frustrated by the inability to get and share information. As a result, the team must be able and prepared to act more like detectives than like surveyors.

5. The due diligence team must communicate within itself. To tackle the due diligence effort, teams are often divided into subgroups. If information is not shared among all subgroups, it's difficult to see the larger issues. Sharing data through regular updates can help identify "deal killers" and allocate resources more effectively.

6. The due diligence team must guard against "analysis paralysis." In larger deals, due diligence can be a complex task involving many people, and teams sometimes find themselves trapped in endless loops of inquiry. Some issues will always remain in doubt, and team leaders must realize when it is time to move on.

All of the above work best when the members of the due diligence team have experience across multiple deals and maintain a degree of continuity and contact with the business case team after the handoff.

Spending time on the tough strategic due diligence questions can yield great benefits, such as validating the purchase price, confirming the deal rationale, shedding more light on sources of value, and establishing the buyer's ability to execute. Passing this rigorous stress test ultimately gives employees, investors, and business partners greater confidence in the merger; it shows them that the strategic intent of the deal makes sense and confirms that they will benefit. In light of the meltdown of late 2008, such confidence is more important than ever.

An insightful business case and strategic due diligence are most helpful during the final stages of negotiations, when the momentum is most intense and when, invariably, some of the thorniest questions must be resolved. Ideas, such as multiple headquarters and advance commitments to certain footprints and to customer promises, can begin to sound reasonable in the heat of eleventh-hour merger negotiations, but not as the morning light dawns over the new company. Both sides need a reference point against which they can check last-minute concessions to ensure that they do not undercut the transaction's strategic intent or harm the integration; strategic due diligence and an enhanced business case provide that reference point.

At the same time, moving through the due diligence stage as quickly as possible is always beneficial. Drawn-out negotiations and extended due diligence can sap the strength of a company's leadership and the deal team alike, increase the risk of deal-threatening leaks, and, of course, frustrate or even dissuade would-be sellers. During these first two stages, how can a team reconcile the intensive need for speed with the expanded complexity of the business case and the increased need for due diligence? The holistic approach to M&A, including a merganic road map and an experienced team, can make all the difference here. The strategic work conducted in preparing a merganic road map ensures that many of the fundamental issues that determine a deal's success are already answered. Well-thought-out capability chains and a robust business case can reduce due diligence time by providing insightful, sharp questions for an alert due diligence team that understands the intent and "soul" of a proposed deal. Well-prepared teams that are not limited to the typical due diligence checklist can provide confidence that the answers are sound.

STAGE 3: PLOTTING THE POSTMERGER INTEGRATION

"All happy families resemble one another, but each unhappy family is unhappy in its own way," wrote Leo Tolstoy. His famous observation could just as easily be applied to acquisition integrations. Successful integration depends on navigating a multitude of complexities that offer a seemingly infinite number of ways to disappoint the participants. Like familial unhappiness, failure can occur in many ways, but there are a number of elements that all successful integration plans have in common.

Integration is successful when all the members of the corporate family are satisfied: management, boards of directors, employees, customers, investors, and business partners. Any of these groups can create stress if its needs, expectations, and desires are not clearly addressed, especially, as is often the case, when they are not completely fulfilled. One Booz & Company survey revealed that this risk rises with the size of the companies involved. In 2007, a second Booz & Company survey of corporate deal makers found that the risk of acquisition failure also rises with the relative size of the target business alone. In fact, as

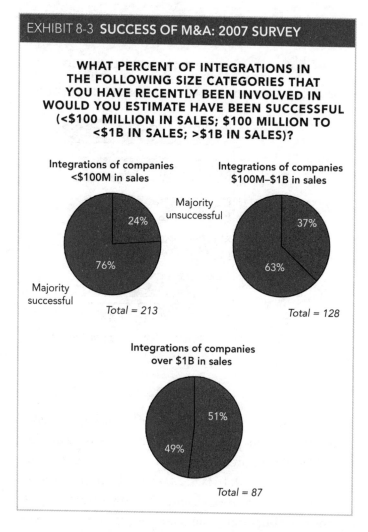

EXHIBIT 8-3 SUCCESS OF M&A: 2007 SURVEY

WHAT PERCENT OF INTEGRATIONS IN THE FOLLOWING SIZE CATEGORIES THAT YOU HAVE RECENTLY BEEN INVOLVED IN WOULD YOU ESTIMATE HAVE BEEN SUCCESSFUL (<$100 MILLION IN SALES; $100 MILLION TO <$1B IN SALES; >$1B IN SALES)?

Integrations of companies <$100M in sales

24%
76%

Majority unsuccessful
Majority successful

Total = 213

Integrations of companies $100M–$1B in sales

37%
63%

Total = 128

Integrations of companies over $1B in sales

51%
49%

Total = 87

Exhibit 8-3 shows, almost half of the largest transactions, in which the target had more than $1 billion in sales, were not successful under the criteria the companies themselves had established.

Early and comprehensive integration planning is essential to managing risk because, although every M&A

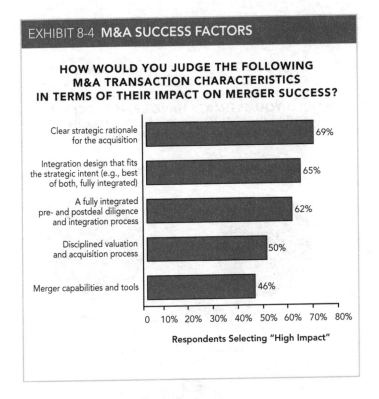

EXHIBIT 8-4 M&A SUCCESS FACTORS

HOW WOULD YOU JUDGE THE FOLLOWING M&A TRANSACTION CHARACTERISTICS IN TERMS OF THEIR IMPACT ON MERGER SUCCESS?

Characteristic	High Impact
Clear strategic rationale for the acquisition	69%
Integration design that fits the strategic intent (e.g., best of both, fully integrated)	65%
A fully integrated pre- and postdeal diligence and integration process	62%
Disciplined valuation and acquisition process	50%
Merger capabilities and tools	46%

Respondents Selecting "High Impact"

failure is unique in its form and details, the highest risk of failure lies in the pre- and postclose planning and the postclose execution of the deal (also known as the post-merger integration). In fact, as seen in Exhibit 8-4, when executives who were experienced in M&A were asked to list the most important characteristics of successful deals, two of the top three factors were directly related to integration planning.

Integration success depends on having an effective planning process that charts the integration function by function, business by business, geography by geography—articulating what each should look like after the merger—

and team by team—articulating what each should be doing to bring the plan to life.

There are ten critical "must dos" (nine team deliverables plus strong program management) during integration planning. These must-dos create strong links back to the business case and due diligence findings. They continue the process of testing, validating, and refining initial assumptions; they also provide detailed, comprehensive "how to" guidance for the integration. Each must-do is a piece of the integration puzzle without which the overall plan is incomplete: it's all too easy to forget a piece, such as stakeholder enthusiasm, and set the stage for acquisition failure. Thus, the best way to deliver on the promise of a merger is to figure out, before the postmerger integration stage begins, exactly how to keep all of the integration teams working against *all* nine deliverables.

1. *Translate strategic intent into integration guidance.* Now that the predeal business case has been converted into the actual terms of an agreement, it is time to convert the rationale for the merger and the goals for the merged company into specific, team by team, integration guidelines. This means formulating answers for differing functions, geographies, and lines of business to questions such as "Is the merger's goal consolidation?" "Is it a vertical integration or an entrée into an adjacent market?" "Does the acquiring company want to transform the entire organization, absorb the merger partner, or simply attach it and allow it to function independently?"

Articulating strategic intent team by team allows the designers of the combined company to see the immediate priorities in integrating systems, people, and processes, and it gives the integration leadership team its marching orders. This requires answering additional questions, such as "Should the team concentrate on how-to steps because senior management already has a design for a particular process, or should it develop alternative design recommendations?" "In which functions should one company absorb the other?" "Which functions should take the time and energy to develop new, improved processes that incorporate the best of both companies' existing best practices?"

Identifying questions such as these early in the integration planning process has two benefits: it creates the clarity teams need to work efficiently, and it forces senior management to come to a common view as to the design and direction of the combined company.

The purchase by R.J. Reynolds (RJR) of Brown & Williamson (B&W) in 2004 for $2.6 billion represented a clearly articulated strategic intent for an acquisition within a single industry (cigarettes). Following a restructuring effort that took $1 billion of costs out of its operations, RJR's acquisition of B&W offered $600 million in synergies and the ability to refocus its product portfolio resources on two key brands (Camel and Kool) with high-growth potential. The company made intensive efforts during this process to communicate the intent, and the possible combined value, to those who would become employees of the combined company, Reynolds American Inc. (RAI). After the merger, the company systematically captured best practices across functions, including approaches to managing retail channels, proprietary methods for collecting consumer information, and general and administrative cost management. In February 2006, RAI's stock hit $105, up from $30 two years before, shortly before the merger.

In 2000, when Pfizer combined with Warner-Lambert in a $90 billion merger, the strategic intent of the deal varied by business and function. As a result, Pfizer's pharmaceutical group absorbed Warner-Lambert's pharmaceutical subsidiary Parke-Davis, while Warner-Lambert's consumer group absorbed the much smaller Pfizer consumer health business.

2. *Build external stakeholder enthusiasm.* In the wake of a merger, it's easy to become consumed by the tumult within the organization, but often the ability to succeed in the long term is shaped by how various external stakeholders respond. All companies worry about customers and shareholders during a merger, but the list of impacted stakeholders is much longer, sometimes including franchisees, supply chain partners, regulators, schools and other sources of talent, local communities, municipal governments, and alliance partners. The integration plan needs to spell out what to say, when to say it, and whom to say it to for each of these constituencies, as well as to lay out specific action plans (what will be done differently for specific stakeholders and what will remain unchanged) as required.

These plans must be made quickly and clearly as part of the overall product, service, and communications strategies in order to build stakeholder enthusiasm. For some stakeholders, the combination will be welcome news. They may gain access to better, broader product lines, integrated solutions, and cost savings. For others, part of the strategy must include assuaging their concerns, both about the short-term impact of the merger, for example, potential job losses in a small town or city, and about the long-term implications, such as for a jittery business partner who might fear being replaced. (This process will be made all the easier if the strategic intent has been clearly articulated.)

Relying only on broadly phrased press releases and bulletins to communicate the deal's story to the outside world is a surefire mistake. Stakeholders scrutinize everything a company says and, just as certainly, everything it does. Service changes and staff repositioning send a clearer message to customers and regulators than the best and most expensive PR campaign. Instead, integration planning should focus first on those stakeholders who are critical to deal success and whose support the company is most at risk of losing, detailing how to reach out to them directly and individually. For those stakeholders who stand to benefit, the integration plan should detail how and when progress will be demonstrated; for those who will be negatively affected by the merger, a plan for mitigating fears by using both advocacy (explaining the purpose for the merger and its benefits for them) and inquiry (learning more fully about their concerns and the reasons the merger has triggered resistance) is needed.

3. *Design "one company."* The challenge of creating one company from two formerly independent, and often competing, organizations is a daunting task. It requires lofty thinking, including a revised philosophy and business model for the new combined company, to pull it off and deliver on the merger's promise. At the same time, it entails sweating the smallest details, such as fulfilling every change notification clause in all existing contracts, or deciding which signs must be changed on which buildings on which days (one company had to delay its launch schedule to arrange to get a helicopter capable of hoisting new letters to the top of its headquarters building).

It is easy to recognize poorly crafted integration plans. They are often too high level, leaving line managers to "figure it out." They capture only the "top ten" interdependencies, not the gritty details, or rely on optimistic assumptions rather than pragmatic realities. The worst plans are simply paper exercises that no one really intends to follow after close. Conversely, a good plan for a positive "one company" outcome describes the necessary changes in organizational structures, systems and processes, and management practices for each business and function at a detailed task level. It specifies how many people the merged company actually needs, which physical locations need to be eliminated, which business partners will be kept, and which incentive structures and business systems can be combined. The plan includes specific milestones as well as defining who will be responsible for each element. Furthermore, the design should ensure that all the proposed function- or business-specific plans are consistent with one another—especially when there are strong interdependencies—and with the original strategic intent.

Finally, the successful one company plan has three major elements: a detailed design for the desired end state, a portrait of where the company should be on Day One, and detailed rendering and sequencing of all of the transition steps between the two points. The detailed sequencing of these steps allows management to validate the costs and timing of implementation and synergy capture. It also helps support groups, such as IT, training, and finance, plan for resource needs in critical path areas.

4. *Capture near-term value; position for upsides.* There is enormous pressure to demonstrate clear progress during the first year or two of a merger. The key to successfully managing that pressure is to provide synergies at the right pace: fast and fierce enough to keep the faith of stakeholders by demonstrating tangible results, but not so aggressive as to sap the new organization of morale, talent, and energy, which would sabotage the merger. Typically, a company has 6 to 12 months to deliver short-term results to its stakeholders in the most obvious areas, such as savings from eliminating redundancies in overlapping support functions and capturing immediate cross-selling opportunities. But short-term synergies represent only the obvious low-hanging fruit. To fully deliver on a merger's promise and unlock the new company's potential, the transition teams must find creative ways to

improve the way business is done—not just folding together the combined companies but rethinking the new company's infrastructure and processes.

Any integration plan that focuses solely on cost reduction runs the risk of planting the seeds for future shareholder discontent. In parallel with looking for cost synergies, the best practitioners also identify growth opportunities and other longer-term upsides. Examining both sides of value capture—savings and upsides—helps a company to avoid short-term cost decisions that could preclude longer-term benefits. For example, the 2006 merger of Linde AG and British Oxygen Company created significant savings in overlapping geographies. However, each company also had unique skills in different industrial gas applications that could be transferred and combined to create valuable long-term growth and differentiation opportunities. As a result, the companies designed an integration plan that balanced global technology investments with regional applications capabilities and, in doing so, created an integration plan that was very different from a plan that focused solely on cost cutting.

Reducing costs is relatively easy, but doing so in the context of strategic intent, stakeholder enthusiasm, and one-company design limitations is far more challenging. The hallmark of the best deal makers is their ability to create plans in which *specific* cost and growth initiatives can be separately tracked as projects, rather than getting lost in the vagaries and ever-shifting components of the P&L. Such plans are also a distinguishing feature of the most successful deals.

5. *Energize the teams.* Building energized and enthusiastic integration teams that draw from the best of both organizations, as appropriate, is a critical planning challenge. Without such teams, the combined company has zero chance of delivering on the merger's promise.

After a deal closes, employees at all levels will continue to be consumed with questions and anxieties about their individual career prospects and choices. Until their concerns are allayed and the benefits of commitment to the combined company are demonstrated, they often will not wholeheartedly support the integration. True buy-in occurs only when employees understand clearly what they are being asked to do and what their opportunities are if they choose to stay. Therefore, the fifth must-do is to get the right employees and managers into the right jobs and to enable them to be enthusiastic about their new roles and about the combined company.

In addition to the selection and retention strategies typically used in acquisitions, this requires that the planning teams identify the people implications associated with the integration plans they have designed and plot a transition path for employees that defines position and skill changes with the same rigor as the business and synergies paths described above. Most companies use top-down culture surveys and comparisons to support vision and values integration, and to flag systemic conditions that may cause people problems during the integration. The best M&A practitioners go a step further. They also do bottom-up initiative-linked change management and culture planning that focuses on the grassroots changes necessary to make the integration design a reality. These "miniculture" projects are part of each integration and synergy initiative; they are short-lived, are well-defined, and have a specific, focused purpose.

Finally, integration planners need to consider the power of the daily hallway chatter among executives and employees, which can either undermine the integration or be harnessed to positive effect. In addition to formal communications, these back channels provide an important avenue for building enthusiasm and excitement; they are also an effective way to defuse the kind of rumor and gossip that can paralyze a workforce.

If employees must constantly read the tea leaves to divine truths about the company's future that they believe their supervisors are unwilling to state openly, they can become anxious. Under such circumstances, even a minor move, like the casual assignment of office space, can bring entire departments to a halt. Sound integration planning recognizes that it is nearly impossible to overcommunicate during a merger. The pipeline will always fill with "information"; the only choice is whether it is leadership that is providing that information.

6. *Stabilize operations.* In the midst of merger-related pressures, distractions, and conflicts, it's easy to lose sight of the acquirer's primary responsibility: keeping both companies going until and after they become one. If operations grind to a halt during integration, the future of the merger is bleak indeed. Integration, planners head off this problem by asking two basic

questions: "Where are the risks to continued business stability?" "What can be done to address these risks—at least on a contingency basis?"

There are four components to a good stability plan. The first is an announcement-day game plan that ensures positive, or at least neutral, reactions, and the second is the Day One (the first day after change of control) communications and outreach plan. Both of these should be familiar to most practitioners. But the final two elements, short-term operating procedures and stability mechanisms, are less obvious.

Short-term operating procedures, the third and possibly most challenging element, help the new company run effectively during the period between closing and actual integration. Especially in the first crucial weeks of a merger, planners need to provide an early sensing ability that sniffs out problems before they grow intractable. Are the products getting placed on the shelves? Is the sales force covering all the stores? Is the company experiencing too much unintended and undesirable talent attrition? To answer these questions, the integration plan should identify the key metrics that provide "canary in the coal mine" warnings and unrelentingly monitor and report progress on these. The CEO of an Australian conglomerate with extensive M&A experience has developed another approach to keeping operations running smoothly. He appoints a "risk management czar," someone who is independent of the business units and reports directly to him. The czar is asked to keep his ear to the ground for threats to the day-to-day business. This is the person who notices that the parking lot is half empty and finds out why.

Fourth, every major transition throughout the life of the implementation—every product rationalization and accounting procedure change—needs its own stability plan and problem-resolution mechanisms. To maintain stable operations, planners need to focus on three primary areas: internal business processes, organizational control, and problem resolution. The plan should detail a set of interim processes and controls, as well as mechanisms for resolving problems, so that no debilitating interruptions in service or staff defections occur. Integration decisions may take some time, but issues such as delegation of authority, payroll, workload conflicts, and pricing must be resolved immediately—if only temporarily—for the organization to function. There might be a merger going on, but everybody still needs to know who their boss is and what their job entails at that moment.

Quest Diagnostics faced these challenges as it integrated a series of acquisitions from the late 1990s to the mid-2000s. Each deal involved combining a complex network of laboratories, physicians, and time-sensitive couriers in a business where customers would switch to competitors if the operation did not continue to operate smoothly through all phases of the integration. The leaders of the company recognized the imperative and spent a great deal of time on the integration plan, conducting what-if scenarios, simulations, and trials before the final implementation.

7. *Close the deal.* The last mile of the merger negotiation marathon is exhausting and fraught with minutiae, legalities, and hard, sometimes emotional, decisions. Yet closing the deal as quickly as possible is critical. A long-drawn-out process can sap the strength of employees, disrupt current operations, and, of course, delay management's ability to deliver on its promises.

The integration planning work and the transaction finalization effort do not live in separate worlds; each influences the other. The work of the integration teams can sometime provide answers or analyses that are useful in responding to regulators' and antitrust authorities' questions, or that can help assuage a nervous seller's concerns about the buyer's intentions. The process of finalizing a deal often influences the pace and sequence of integration planning by "gating" data sharing across the companies or by creating other limitations or commitments that the integration team has to design around. For one U.S.-based merger, the integration team had to modify its layoff plans in one state because the seller's CEO was being considered for a high-level political appointment. He worried that the layoffs might jeopardize this, since it had to be approved by a government committee headed by the affected state's congressional representative.

8. *Identify and manage moments of truth.* For a merger to succeed, it's critical to recognize the big decisions that lie ahead for the new company, decisions that will help determine the organization's strategic course and its implementation effectiveness after the merger or acquisition. All the planning in the world doesn't

make a difference until these tough choices are actually made. These moments of truth often involve very emotional issues, such as the location of a new headquarters, the choice of which factories to close, or the selection of a new corporate name.

But moments of truth also come in more subtle, seemingly minor, ways that only the integration teams—teams close to the companies' cultures and the changes proposed—can identify. In one example, two companies with strong plant safety heritages came together. The smaller company had a policy banning mobile phone use while driving company vehicles (even when it was legal). The new firm adopted that policy. An astute integration team alerted the acquiring company's senior management to the signals their decision would send about the new company's seriousness about safety, and also that this announcement would be seen as an indication of the extent to which the deal was a merger versus an absorption.

Moments of truth can communicate more to the organization and the external world than formal communications, especially when there is a perception that formal statements don't fully reflect management's real intent. Proactively identifying and managing them is a powerful tool for senior leaders and an important task for integration planners.

9. *Create a postclose transition plan.* The final stage of the M&A process is focused on postclose management and avoiding the risks of "drift." But the success of that effort is grounded in robust transition thinking from the integration planning teams and the creation of

transition plans that include detailed integration and synergy capture tasks, explicit execution responsibilities, and guidance as to the who and when of handoffs. Transition plans describe when an initiative is ready for the shift from the integration of the merging companies to the resumption of normalized operations. This includes important decisions, such as when day-to-day line management will take over operations from the dedicated integration teams. A premature return to normal operations can undermine success—but if the handoff is delayed too long, the line managers might not buy into the new plan.

The transition plan serves as the bridge between planning and execution. It describes how to handle differing situations, such as the rapid close (where integration plans may not be fully baked) versus the extended close that allows for more robust, ready-to-go handoffs and for greater continuity, or how to handle the implications of leadership changes from the planning to the execution phase.

Beyond normal good practices, these nine planning deliverables help companies navigate the five trends influencing M&A. Strategic intent helps keep the teams grounded in times of flux and bubbles. Stakeholder enthusiasm forces teams to think in nontraditional as well as traditional ways about stakeholders in an era of strong financial players and new competitors from emerging markets. Compelling one-company and value capture stories with clear end states can help buy investor and employee patience in an era of growing impatience. Operational sta-

CRAFTING THE SUCCESSFUL DEAL

bility and the ability to avoid drift are valuable qualities in a high-velocity, change-driven environment.

Merger integration is never easy, but breaking it down into nine critical "must do's" can make it possible. (A tenth imperative, generally recognized in conventional M&A practice, is rigorous program management.) And the ability to execute difficult mergers, which depends so much on this planning stage, can effectively differentiate a company from competitors and win customers, talent, and shareholders.

STAGE 4: EXECUTING SUCCESSFUL INTEGRATIONS

By the time a company reaches this stage of the merger process, it has conducted an enormous amount of due diligence and has created detailed integration plans. It has considered all the "what if" scenarios and has created alternative plans to manage them. However, like the well-coached, properly assembled football team, the players still have to execute and score in order to win. For the deal promises to become reality, the company has to convert plans into results. This is the work of Stage 4.

Stage 4 is about staying the course after the excitement of the deal has subsided. Beyond the obvious (committing the right people and right level of resources, postclose tracking and measurement, and demanding accountability), the most significant risk to a well-designed implementation plan is drift.

In a business world that increasingly values decentralization and the empowerment of line managers, keeping a complex, interdependent implementation plan on course can be a challenge. It requires adherence to the designed plan, yet also requires that managers be granted the flexibility needed to adapt to changing circumstances. Stage 3 created detailed implementation milestones and responsibilities. But in a decentralized or functionally organized company, the challenge is to decide who can change the plan and under what conditions, and to have a good understanding of how changes in one area may have ripple effects on other areas. Postclose governance issues such as these are neglected far too often.

Postclose governance demands a team with the authority to manage, to enforce plan execution, and to oversee plan variations. While that team may be the executive or management committee, in some cases, a separate, dedicated integration oversight team is necessary to support senior management in its oversight role during the postclose period. That team needs to have some continuity from the business case through due diligence through integration planning, so that it is working from more than a list of tasks and red/yellow/green flags. The team has to have a gut feel for how the integration is progressing in much the same way a mother can sense when a child is becoming ill long before symptoms are evident. To the extent that line managers were deeply involved in integration plan development, they may have the innate sense necessary, but in many situations, there is a handoff to managers who were not previously involved in a substantive sense.

Avoiding drift also requires staying true to the plan when facing difficult decisions. Clarity around strategic intent, especially in the planning stage of a deal, provides a touchstone that carries all the way into this final stage.

Germany's Henkel Corporation, the global household products company, offers a good example. When Henkel undertook its $2.9 billion acquisition of Dial Corporation in 2003 (the deal was concluded in April 2004), the management teams of the two companies had to resolve very different visions of the integration, which could have easily derailed the execution.

"Dial's management knew that they would become part of the bigger Henkel organization, but they were hoping to be left to operate the business as they had in the past. However, at Henkel, the businesses Dial is in—home care and personal care—are managed in different divisions. To avoid adding complexity to Henkel globally, we decided to align Dial with these existing divisions," explains Henkel CFO Lothar Steinebach. "There was a lot of friction. In the end, we had to make clear that the integration plan was not up for negotiation. . . . This kind of resistance isn't unusual in mergers. In the interest of quick and successful integration, you often have to make difficult or unpopular decisions that might even cause some managers to leave. However, when doing so is the only way to ensure a consistent integration strategy, it pays off in the long run."

Unfortunately, the necessary measures are often painful for stakeholders. But not heeding them, and not making the purposeful decisions needed to resolve them, is dangerous. For example, the longer that companies put off decisions regarding how and when to integrate IT systems, the worse the problems associated with incompatibility and the costs of multiple platforms can become, especially in transaction-processing, platform-centric businesses such as banks and insurance companies. When Henkel purchased Dial, Dial was in the first phase of a major enterprise software implementation, which could not be integrated with Henkel's IT system. Henkel decided that the first phase would have to be completed in order to avoid disrupting Dial's business but then, a second implementation, a considerable effort, would have to be undertaken in order to create a consistent IT architecture across the combined companies.

"The IT decision is always tricky," says Steinebach. "I don't even think it's necessary to always make the same decision. You do what is best based on the facts at your disposal, then move ahead. If it turns out that it's not the ideal decision as new information becomes available, you can make adjustments later."

IT is not the only area where unwillingness to follow through on difficult decisions frequently occurs. Plant closings, product line rationalization, and entrenched business practices can all be opportunities for drift.

An on-course implementation also requires "knowing thyself" and the internal characteristics and tendencies that can take implementation off course. Anyone starting a diet is well advised to know those foods that are impossible for them to resist, and when quitting cigarettes, a smoker needs to understand the situations which produce a craving to light up. In an integration, knowing thyself means understanding the cultural tendencies of the company—"we always come back to cost cutting" or "we will always defer to local management"—and how those tendencies can divert a company away from its intended plan. Very successful companies have invested time and resources to build strong core cultures and coherent capabilities. But those source of strength can also be barriers when integration of another company requires change and flexibility.

For example, the transition team leaders in a growth-oriented, high-margin company must recognize and adjust for the fact that its culture and management may not be prepared for an integration that requires substantial cost cutting. Knowing thyself also involves knowing when certain functions or groups tend to dominate in a company (even achieving "untouchable" status), and recognizing that these groups must be addressed head on to maintain momentum.

A well-managed execution is as much a matter of attitude and relationship as it is of process and procedure. Managers must face moments of truth bravely without making short-term decisions or compromises that will impede the integration and long-term value capture. The more the success of the merger is premised on significant change and new approaches, the more important this becomes.

Facing moments of truth, staying focused on the business case, and communicating achievement of the benchmarks set forth in the integration plan can all help in turning two once-independent companies into one coherent organization. And typically, a certain momentum takes hold. The systems and processes, management, and lines of business start folding together. Physical locations close, some people are reassigned, others may be promoted, business partners are chosen, IT systems are linked or eliminated, incentive structures are combined, and cultures are harmonized. In short, the two companies become one, the process of the acquisition is completed, and the new company turns its attention, once again, to the prospects of merganic growth.

SETTING THE STAGE
FOR SUCCESS

Acquisitions and other related corporate development deals offer a myriad of opportunities for failure. This has never been truer than in today's hyperactive environment. Globalization, velocity, new competitors, and speculative bubbles and their consequences can make any mistake more debilitating.

Managing the deal process in a concurrent and integrated fashion—facing moments of truth honestly, communicating clearly, setting benchmarks, all while keeping day-to-day operations running—can sound a lot like common sense. Maybe so, but that doesn't make the task any easier. Pulling all these elements together into a successful execution, under tremendous time and competitive pressures, takes skill and talent. The team of the future is not a separate "development of deal" team. It is deeply involved in the business unit and corporate strategic planning that creates merganic road maps. It builds enhanced business cases and carries that understanding through strategic due diligence, planning, and early implementation. It captures and internalizes a deep understanding—not just playbooks—of what worked in a deal and what could have been done better. And it embeds that understanding in improved road maps as it undertakes the next deal cycle. The companies that master these capabilities and build these teams will be the most successful in the uncertain, hyperactive M&A environment of the coming years.

EPILOGUE:
A MESSAGE TO
LEADING EXECUTIVES

This book begins and ends with the notion that, for any successful company, there is a merge ahead. Continued success depends upon growth, which will inevitably mean capable and well-executed mergers and acquisitions, integrated into a holistic, merganic corporate strategy.

Profitable growth has always been an overriding goal for any business leader. For public companies, it is the key to shareholder value creation. For not-for-profit companies, it is also their lifeblood, best summarized by a client CEO's comment, "No money, no mission!" Fulfilling the demand for profitable growth in the coming years will be as challenging a task as it has been anytime in the past half-century or more.

Chief among the obstacles to growth are the trends we have described in these pages. The collapse of the subprime credit bubble in 2008 and 2009 created a recessionary wave—often described as an economic tsunami—that continued accelerating through the final quarter of 2008 and had already reshaped the global economy by the year's end. The pace of change has become permanently hyperactive as companies are driven to attain capabilities and scale, emerging markets beckon, and powerful new entrants and deep-pocketed financial buyers cast a wider net for growth opportunities. The margin for error has shrunk as the velocity of capital and information has increased the impatience of corporate stakeholders.

In these conditions, leaders must embrace and employ every means to create value and to sustain profitable growth. They must teach their companies to think in merganic terms—maintaining a well-designed combination of organic initiatives, alliances, and M&A.

When companies are successful at adopting a merganic approach, developing a corporate capability for M&A, and directing individual deals—in short, when they are prepared for the merge ahead—they will be more effective at serving their customers, employees, and shareholders, as well as the communities where they operate. For when the quality of M&A and merganic growth in general rises, so does the quality of all corporate performance and results.

Even at the most turbulent moments of 2008, it was clear that the circumstances of the economic tsunami, which included low-growth outlooks and depressed corporate valuations, had created attractive opportunities for mergers and acquisitions. In some sectors, such as financial services, natural resources, and health, there were opportunities of historic proportion—and almost equal risk.

Companies must find ways to match their strategies to the new economic environment in order to survive and prosper. This, in turn, will require building a merganic approach into the fabric of corporate strategy.

A number of leading executives, besides the CEO, are closely involved in developing and instilling a merganic strategy and ensuring its success. The chief financial officer (CFO) oversees the basic financial processes, but also plays a critical role as one of the lead merger strategists and as the leading postclose "scorekeeper." The chief human resources officer will increasingly be called upon to solidify the synergies and complementary capabilities of the talent pools in both merging organizations. The chief information officer and the heads of operations will need to continue implementing the changes from the merger, long after other functions have returned to business as usual. And there is a tremendous need for someone to act as the integration leader. Finally, internal and external stakeholders must be provided with a compelling case if they are to understand and support a company's M&A strategy: its deals, divestitures, and acquisitions. And given today's cacophonous 24×7 high-bandwidth world, in which everyone has an opinion and access to a platform to broadcast it, it is harder than ever to be heard. Someone needs to take on the daunting role of chief communicator or spokesperson.

Thus, savvy executives are integrating corporate development capabilities into every major company's overall approach to M&A. But the strategic recognition of the M&A imperative is just half of the equation. Mastering the art and science of M&A will require the same kind of rigorous and consistent efforts needed to develop any capability, whether it be global talent management, innovation, or Six Sigma. Knowing that there is a merge ahead is the easy part. The path can be navigated only in practice. No one has all the answers; there is still much to be learned from experience, and the winning companies are already racing along the learning curve.

NOTES

Chapter 1

22–23 "Organizations learn in response to competition . . .":
William P. Barnett, *The Red Queen among Organizations: How Competitiveness Evolves* (Princeton, N.J.: Princeton University Press, 2008), pp 44-45.

Chapter 2

30 "The size of a company can be measured in assets, market value of shares, or the size of the workforce . . .": Alfred D. Chandler, Jr., *Scale and Scope: The Dynamics of Industrial Capitalism* (Cambridge, Mass.: Harvard University Press, 1990), pp. 15–17.

32 "As *New York Times* foreign affairs columnist Thomas Friedman proclaimed in his bestselling 2005 book . . .": Thomas Friedman, *The World Is Flat: A Brief History of the Twenty-First Century* (New York: Farrar, Straus and Giroux, 2006).

32 "As Exhibit 2.2 shows, there were at least 17 multibillion-dollar deals in 2006 and 2007 . . .": Joe Saddi, Karim Sabbagh, and Richard Shediac, "Oasis Economies," *strategy+business*, Spring 2008.

35 "Instead of being global, most companies that succeed are highly regional . . .": Art Kleiner, "Pankaj Ghemawat: The Thought Leader Interview," *strategy+business*, Spring 2008.

35 "Our semiglobal world is not yet a fully integrated multinational environment . . .": Pankaj Ghemawat, *Redefining Global Strategy: Crossing Borders in a World Where Differences Still Matter* (Boston, Mass.: Harvard Business School Press, 2007).

40 "As Asaf Farashuddin, the vice president of corporate strategy at the automobile components manufacturer Visteon, told the Booz researchers . . .": Barry Jaruzelski and Kevin Dehoff, "Beyond Borders: The Global Innovation 1000," *strategy+business*, Winter 2008.

44 "Had they given more weight to the mockery, Gillette's innovators . . .": A. G. Lafley and Ram Charan, *The Game-Changer: How You Can Drive Revenue and Profit Growth with Innovation* (New York: Crown Business, 2008).

44 "Pfizer had learned to use its skills in consumer insight and clinical testing to create scientifically backed claims . . .": Cesare Mainardi, Paul Leinwand, and Steffen Lauster, "How to Win by Changing the Game," *strategy+business*, Winter 2008, p. 22.

Chapter 3

52 "The Red Queen Syndrome breeds urgency in decision making . . .": William P. Barnett, *The Red Queen among Organizations: How Competitiveness Evolves* (Princeton, N.J.: Princeton University Press, 2008).

62 "An ongoing Booz & Company study found that annual rates of turnover of CEOs across the globe . . .": Per-Ola Karlsson, Gary L. Neilson, and Juan Carlos Webster, "CEO Succession 2007: The Performance Paradox," *strategy+business*, Summer 2008; http://www.strategy-business.com/press/article/08208.

68 "Recalls former SmithKline Beecham CFO Andrew Bonfield . . .": Robert Hertzberg and Ilona Steffen, eds., *The CFO as Deal Maker: Thought Leaders on M&A Success* (New York: strategy+business Books, 2008), p. 73.

Chapter 4

69 "In broader terms, from the early 1990s to the mid-2000s, the total number of multinational companies whose parents were based in Brazil, China, India, and the Republic of Korea . . .": U.N. Conference on Trade and Development, "World Investment Report 2006," p. 122; http://www.unctad.org/en/docs/wir2006_en.pdf.

69 "The Middle East and South Africa have also launched companies with global aspirations . . .": Joe Saddi, Karim Sabbagh, and Richard Shediac, "Oasis Economies," *strategy+business*, Spring 2008; http://www.strategy-business.com/press/article/08105?pg=all.

71 "Steven Wallace, Citigroup's head of M&A for the Asia-Pacific region, might have been speaking about companies around the world . . .": Nisha Gopalan, "Asia Defies Slump in Mergers," *Wall Street Journal*, June 30, 2008, p. C3.

81 "All of this made InBev a pathfinder . . .": Adapted from José Gregorio Baquero and Paolo Pigorini, "The Beer Case," in Mike Sisk and Andy Sambrook, eds., *The Whole Deal: Fulfilling the Promise of Acquisitions and Mergers* (New York: strategy+business Books, 2006), pp. 236–237.

82 "The middle-class population in Argentina, for instance, doubled from 2003 to 2007; . . .": "Adiós to Poverty, Hola to Consumption," *The Economist*, August 18, 2007, pp. 21–23.

85 "By recognizing this general pattern and identifying where a country currently fits into it . . .": For more information on the evolution of markets, see Alonso Martinez and Ronald Haddock, "The Flatbread Factor," *strategy+business*, Spring 2007; http://www.strategy-business.com/press/article/07106?pg=all.

91 "A lot of mergers fail because . . .": Robert Hertzberg and Ilona Steffen, eds., *The CFO as Deal Maker: Thought Leaders on M&A Success* (New York: strategy+business Books, 2008), p. 156.

91–92 "We built a beautiful Roman Orthodox church . . .": ibid., p. 28.

92 "The sharing of best practice between our very enthusiastic and hugely talented Korean colleagues and others . . .": "Standard Chartered Marks 30th June as Korea Day," Standard Chartered, June 29, 2005; http://www.standardchartered .com/gm/mc/news/2005/pdf_gm_30062005.pdf.

93 "Still others, as management writer C .K. Prahalad suggests, may reduce . . .": C. K. Prahalad and Hrishi Bhattacharyya, "20 Hubs and No HQ," *strategy+business*, Spring 2008.

Chapter 5

96 "'Chrysler Deal Heralds New Direction for Detroit,' announced the page one story . . .": Gina Chon, Jason Singer, and Jeffrey McCracken, *Wall Street Journal*, May 15, 2007.

96 "We don't think about what analysts have to say about us . . .": "Chrysler Group to Be Sold for $7.4 Billion," Associated Press, May 14, 2007; http://www.msnbc.msn.com/ id/18645179/.

99–100 "In the United States, for example, PE firms Carlyle Group and Apollo Management . . .": Figures from the firms.

101 "In 2006, these wealthy individuals globally allocated 10 percent of their portfolios . . .": "World Wealth Report 2007," Capgemini/Merrill Lynch, 2007, pp. 2, 15; http://www.ml .com/media/79882.pdf.

101 "'Private equity firms embarked on one of the biggest spending sprees in corporate history for nearly three years . . .'": Andrew Ross Sorkin and Michael J. de la Merced, "Debt Linked to Buyouts Tightens Economic Vise," *New York Times*, November 3, 2008; http://www.nytimes.com/2008/11/03/ business/economy/03equity.html.

102 "As a result, at the beginning of 2007, close to 14,000 firms worldwide . . .": About 80 percent of the study group included traditional private equity deals involving a financial sponsor; leveraged management buyouts made up the remaining 20 percent. "The Global Economic Impact of Private Equity Report 2008," World Economic Forum, 2008, p. viii.

102 "Sovereign wealth funds are estimated to control . . .": Landon Thomas, Jr., "Cash-Rich, Publicity-Shy, Abu Dhabi Fund Draws Scrutiny," *New York Times*, February 28, 2008; http://www.nytimes.com/2008/02/28/business/worldbusiness/28fund.html; "Sovereign Wealth Funds," International Financial Services London, April 2008, p. 1.

103 "In the first three quarters of 2007, these five Middle Eastern funds . . .": Stephen Grocer, "The Middle East: Quenching Its M&A Thirst," *WallStreetJournal.com*, September 20, 2007; http://blogs.wsj.com/deals/2007/09/20/the-middle-east-quenching-its-ma-thirst/.

108 "India alone saw total investment increase 700 percent . . .": "Global Economic Impact of Private Equity Report 2008," pp. xi, 16.

108 "Given the economic growth rates. . .": Donald Greenlees, "In Asia, Private Equity Is Still Bullish," *New York Times*, September 4, 2007; http://www.nytimes.com/2007/09/04/business/worldbusiness/04equity.html.

109 "Said David Rubenstein, cofounder of the Carlyle Group, in 2007 . . .": "Carlyle to Boost Efforts in China," *China Daily*, November 15, 2007; http://www.chinadaily.com.cn/bizchina/2007-11/15/content_6256892.htm.

112 "Additionally, there were also Little Sheep restaurants . . .": "Global Economic Impact of Private Equity Report 2008," pp. 131–136.

112 "In March 2009, U.S. Operator Yum! Brands . . . ": "Yum! Takes $63 Million Bite of China's Little Sheep," Reuters, March 25, 2009; http://u.k.reuters.com/article/innovationNews/idUKTRES2017920090325.

114 "The increase in patent importance, as denoted by patent citations . . .": "Global Economic Impact . . . ," p. xi.

Chapter 6

120 "And you'll see much more overseas activity from the private equity firms . . .": "Carlyle Group's David Rubenstein: 'The

Greatest Period for Private Equity Is Probably Ahead of Us,'"
Knowledge@Wharton, May 6, 2008; http://knowledge.wharton
.upenn.edu/article.cfm?articleid=1957.

123 "Similar patterns can be seen in other regions . . .": Robert J.
Borghese and Paul Borgese, *M&A from Planning to Integration:
Executing Acquisitions and Increasing Shareholder Value* (New
York: McGraw-Hill, 2002).

126 "At least one academic study has shown that companies in
which executives accomplish this . . .": Gerry McNamara, Jer-
ayr Haleblian, and Bernadine Johnson Dykes, "The Performance Implications of Participating in an Acquisition Wave:
Early Mover Advantages, Bandwagon Effects, and the Moder-
ating Influence of Industry Characteristics and Acquirer Tactics," *Academy of Management Journal*, February 2008.

130 "There is an escalation in public knowledge of the arguments . . .": Robert J. Shiller, *The Subprime Solution: How Today's Global Financial Crisis Happened, and What to Do about It*
(Princeton, N.J.: Princeton University Press, 2008), pp. 41–47.

131 "A report at the time by Booz & Company and the World Eco-
nomic Forum . . .": Booz Allen Hamilton and World Economic
Forum Automotive Board of Governors, *A Biofuelled Future?*
(World Economic Forum, 2007); Eric Spiegel and Neil
McArthur, *Energy Shift: Game-Changing Options for Fueling the
Future* (New York: McGraw-Hill, 2009), pp 69–74.

Chapter 7

140 "The second reason why organic growth alone tends not to be
sustainable . . .": William P. Barnett, *The Red Queen among Organizations: How Competitiveness Evolves* (Princeton, N.J.:
Princeton University Press, 2008).

142 "'Capabilities are the particular ideas, skills and competen-
cies . . .'": Cesare Mainardi, Paul Leinwand, and Steffen
Lauster, "How to Win by Changing the Game," *strategy+business*,
Winter 2008, p. 22.

144 "For example, in 1955, GE's newfound ability . . .": Franklin Friday, *A Walk through the Park: The History of GE Appliances and Appliance Park* (Louisville, Ky.: Elfun Historical Society, 1987).

151 "As the famous quote (originally by American psychologist Abraham Maslow) put it . . .": Abraham Maslow, *Psychology of Science* (New York: Harper & Row, 1966), p. 15.

152 "This was our biggest transaction . . .": Robert Hertzberg and Ilona Steffen, eds., *The CFO as Deal Maker: Thought Leaders on M&A Success* (New York: strategy+business Books, 2008), pp. 55–56.

155 "In fact, through early March 2008, Fox . . .": Paul R. La Monica, *Inside Rupert's Brain* (New York: Portfolio, 2009), p. 56.

Chapter 8

170 "'They were strong where we were weak . . .'": Robert Hertzberg and Ilona Steffen, eds., *The CFO as Deal Maker: Thought Leaders on M&A Success* (New York: strategy+business Books, 2008), pp. 132–133.

174 "'Of course you have to have a good grip on the financials . . .'": ibid., p. 111.

197 "However, when doing so is the only way . . .": ibid, pp. 122–123.

198 "'If it turns out that it's not the ideal decision . . .'": ibid, p. 128.

INDEX

ABOUT THE AUTHORS

GERALD ADOLPH (gerald.adolph@booz.com) is a New York-based senior partner with Booz & Company. He leads the firm's work for mergers and restructuring clients.

Gerald's work primarily focuses on assisting clients with growth strategy, new business development, and industry restructuring. He has led multiple M&A predeal assessments, as well as complex and challenging multibillion-dollar postmerger integration assignments in the pharmaceutical, consumer products, health services, agribusiness, chemicals, telecom, and financial services industries. He is a recipient of Booz & Company's Professional Excellence Award, which was given in recognition of outstanding and innovative client service on a merger-related client engagement.

A recognized thought leader in his field, Gerald is a regular guest commentator on CNBC. His writing and commentary have been published in *strategy+business*, *The Deal*, *Corporate Dealmaker*, *Business Finance*, *CFO magazine*, and Harvard Business School's *Working Knowledge*.

Gerald has served as a member of Booz & Company's board of directors, leader of the firm's global chemicals business, and leader of the firm's global consumer and health practice. He holds an MBA from the Harvard Business School, as well as a Master's degree in chemical engineering from the Massachusetts Institute of Technology. He also holds BS degrees in chemical engineering and in management science/organizational psychology from MIT.

JUSTIN PETTIT (justin.pettit@booz.com) is a New York-based partner with Booz & Company who specializes in corporate finance and shareholder value. With more than 15 years of strategy and corporate finance advisory experience as an investment banker and management consultant, he brings a uniquely practical perspective to the issues and applications of modern corporate finance. He advises boards of directors and senior executives on valuation and corporate strategy, acquisitions, divestitures and major capital decisions, capital markets issues, optimal capital structure, and financial risk management.

Justin is the author of *Strategic Corporate Finance: Applications in Valuation & Capital Structure* (New York: Wiley, 2007). A highly ranked author on the Social Sciences Research Network (ssrn.com), his articles and reviews have appeared in *Harvard Business Review*, *strategy+business*, *Journal of Applied Corporate Finance*, *Corporate Finance Review*, *Industrial Management*, *Business Quarterly*, *Shareholder Value Magazine*, *Air Finance Journal*, *Financier Worldwide*, *Financial Executive*, *Journal of Pension Economics and Finance*, and *Quantitative Finance*.

A popular guest lecturer in advanced corporate finance at business schools, seminars, and public conferences, including the Brookings Institute, the Financial Management Association, and Finance Executives Institute, Justin holds an MBA from the University of Western Ontario and a BSc in mechanical engineering from the University of Toronto.

MICHAEL SISK (michaelasisk@yahoo.com) is a New York-based business writer and editor who has covered the financial markets and business management issues for 15 years, including stints as the investor editor at *Red Herring* and editor-at-large at *US Banker*. His articles have appeared in numerous publications, including *Barron's, Crain's New York Business, Institutional Investor, strategy+ business, Harvard Management Update,* and *Worth*.

Michael helped write and edit two previous books, *The Whole Deal: Fulfilling the Promise of Acquisitions and Mergers* (strategy+business Books, 2006) and *Wealth: How the World's High-Net-Worth Grow, Sustain and Manage Their Fortunes* (Canada: Wiley, 2008). He holds a BA from Haverford College and an MSJ from Northwestern University's Medill School of Journalism.

ACKNOWLEDGMENTS

THIS BOOK, and the entire Future of Business series, has been a rewarding exercise in collaboration. Our first editor and publisher at McGraw-Hill, Herb Schaffner, helped instigate this project and drive it forward. Our new editor, Editorial Director Mary Glenn, carried it to fruition. As with the three previous books in this series, we continued to enjoy the benefits of working with McGraw-Hill's production team, especially Production Manager Ruth Mannino, Editorial Coordinator Ed Chupak, and Junior Designer Ty Nowicki.

The contributions of many outstanding individuals at Booz & Company were instrumental in the development of our thinking and this book. Andrew Sambrook, the book's original project manager, contributed impetus, knowledge, perspective, and oversight. Many insights were gleaned from client project work with our colleagues Karla Elrod and J. Neely, and from Marina Hervy's research. We benefited from interviews with and critique by Tom Casey, from Thomas Flaherty's ideas on velocity and impatience, and from the insights of our colleagues who worked with us on *The CFO as Deal Maker: Thought Leaders on M&A Success* (strategy+business Books, 2008), including Irmgard Heinz, Jens Niebuhr, Klaus Mattern, and Ilona Steffen. We are grateful to Kate Pinkerton for helping us bring this project to a successful conclusion, and to Adrienne Crowther, Brian Gorin, Nigel Andrews, Michael Eckstut, and Rhonda Germany, whose work over the years provided a foundation for the merganic road map approach. We also wish to acknowledge the critical support for this project of colleagues at Booz & Company, particularly (but not limited to) Shumeet Banerji, Joe Saddi, Cesare Mainardi, Paul Leinwand, Barry Jaruzelski, Karim Sabbagh, Klaus-Peter Gushurst, and Tom Stewart.

Merge Ahead was developed and edited under the auspices of *strategy+business*, the quarterly magazine published by our firm. We would like to thank publisher Jonathan Gage, who helped conceive the series and its promotion; literary agent Jim Levine, who introduced us to McGraw-Hill; and publicist Mark Fortier and marketing manager Alan Shapiro, who have helped make the book visible. Art Kleiner, editor-in-chief of *strategy+business*, provided editorial oversight and clarity, and Senior Editor Theodore Kinni provided valuable assistance.

strategy+business

The Wall Street Journal bestseller!

Always On • Vollmer

"Always On *captures the essence of how the Internet is putting control in the hands of consumers, and offers straightforward guidance for executives and companies to not only survive but thrive in that world as it changes.*"

—Dave Morgan, founder of RealMedia and Tacoda; former EVP of Global Advertising Strategy for AOL

Learn more. Do more.
MHPROFESSIONAL.COM

Available everywhere books are sold

strategy+business

The Wall Street Journal bestseller!

Make or Break · Grichnik

"Make or Break *goes beyond Lean and footprint optimization.
This is the book to read before starting to reinvent your
next-generation manufacturing."*

—**Thierry Chiche, vice president of manufacturing, Michelin Europe**

Learn more. Do more.
MHPROFESSIONAL.COM

Available everywhere books are sold

strategy+business

Are you prepared for the energy shift?

Energy Shift • Spiegel

"Energy Shift provides a comprehensive, well-balanced review of the complex world of energy issues—its clear facts and insights make it a very good read for any senior executive."

—Lodewijk van Wachem, former president of Royal Dutch/Shell

Learn more. Do more.
MHPROFESSIONAL.COM

Available everywhere books are sold